TASSELS

The Fanciful Embellishment

TASSELS

The Fanciful Embellishment

NANCY WELCH

Lark
Books

Published in 1992 by Lark Books

Altamont Press
50 College Street
Asheville, North Carolina, U.S.A., 28801

Editors: Eric Carlson, Chris Rich
Art Director: Sandra Montgomery
Illustrations: Gail Gandolfi
Production: Sandra Montgomery, Elaine Thompson, Charlie Covington

ISBN 1-887374-23-X

Library of Congress Cataloging-in-Publication Data
Welch, Nancy.
    Tassels : the fanciful embellishment / by Nancy Welch.
        p.   cm.
    Includes bibliographical references and index.
    ISBN 1-887374-23-X
    1. Tassels.   I. Title.
TT899.5.W46   1992
746.2'7--dc20   91-34630
                                                                              CIP

First Edition

10 9 8 7 6 5 4 3 2

Printed in Hong Kong

Table of Contents

Tassels: The Fanciful Embellishment

Introduction

Have you ever bought something that you really liked, but for which you had absolutely no use? You just knew you had to have it, and now every time you see it or touch it or think about it, it brings you pleasure.

Suppose for a moment that this "something" has existed, in one form or another, for centuries. Imagine that millions of people from cultures circling the world have enjoyed it, although none of them have had a use for it either. Sound absurd? Could there really be such a thing? Consider the tassel.

When I mention tassels, people respond with anything from a blank stare to a giggle. Most will quickly recall a tassel hanging on an old window shade or swinging elsewhere in their memories. The woman who giggled when I mentioned tassels confided that in her family a tassel referred to one part of the male anatomy. This certainly added a new dimension to my premise that tassels are purely for pleasure!

Whatever your ideas about tassels may be, I hope to add to your pleasure through an appreciation of a universal art form that until now has received little recognition. Tassels provide a glimpse of the range of human creativity unburdened by the need for function. Tassel designers are free to investigate any and all materials and processes. I'd like to share my discoveries and to offer new challenges and opportunities for exploring the wonderful world of tassels.

This book is not intended to be the definitive work on tassels. I hope that book will never be written. There will always be new techniques to try, new knots and braids, new yarns and materials, and always new people to add a special twist to tassels. I hope this book will inspire you to be one of those people. Please keep in touch. I'd love to hear your tassel tales and see your discoveries. The history and scope of this art form have barely been touched. If tassels are the thread that binds us all together, perhaps together we can create the complete tassel story.

Victorian trimmings courtesy of Scalamandré

Tassels: The Fanciful Embellishment

The World of Tassels

How did it all begin? It's hard to believe that God just said, "Let there be tassels!" Yet the Bible does make specific references to their use, a use that continues in many religions today. Or perhaps tassels originated when an early weaver said, "Let there be an end to this mess!" and tied up the loose threads, inventing a technique that simultaneously ended raveling and created the tassel. Whatever their origin, tassels quickly outgrew their function of controlling unruly ends and became separate artistic forms.

From the dawn of civilization to the present day, man has added decoration to both the grandest and most humble of his possessions, but perhaps no single form of ornament has been as widely used for as many centuries as the tassel. The opulent silk tassels found in the surroundings of royalty have their counterparts in the rugged wool hangings of nomadic people. Tassels may hang in a palace or a yurt; be of the finest thread or the coarsest goat hair; be relics of antiquity or brand-new decorations.

Whatever the material, manner of construction, or ultimate destination, tassels share but one aim—to capture the fancy of those who behold them. Superfluous? Yes, yet amazingly they have survived throughout history with no practical function. They exist solely to provide that certain flair, that note of elegance, playfulness, or special significance, that final touch to all they adorn. A tassel is the exclamation point of a textile sentence.

Victorian tieback

Tassels on parade

S o how do we go about stalking these superfluous objects? Like so many things in life, once you become aware of them, tassels will seem to find you, popping up when least expected. You'll discover them hanging in the windows of cottages and castles, as well as in motels and motor homes. They perch jauntily on car antennas, sway from rearview mirrors, flutter from flags, keep time on marching band uniforms, and were even found bobbing and weaving on world heavyweight champion Muhammad Ali's boxing shoes!

Tassels adorn animals in parades and circuses and often appear on farm animals at work in the fields. In Peru, animals are blessed by placing tassels in their hair.

You'll spot tassels in churches, at dances, and in theaters, where they grace both stage and performer alike. They play an important role in Chinese opera, where heroes are distinguished from villains by the color of the tassels they wear, and where wild-flying tasseled sticks represent horses.

In the Ryukyu Islands of Japan, men used tassels on their belts as calculators. Threads were divided between the fingers to keep track of the total count (the ones, between the thumb and forefinger; the tens, between

forefinger and middle finger, etc.).

Tassels also figure prominently in religion. Jewish law specifies tassels on prayer shawls as a reminder to obey God's commandments. Ecclesiastical garments are often accented with tassels. They designate rank on the heraldry of Catholic clergy and add power to a shaman's magic.

Tassels are no longer merely a means of controlling unruly ends, and while most tassels swing and sway, some are solid and stiff. We find the latter anywhere from tomb carvings to Tiffany jewels. Tassels may be fashioned from wood, metal, and ivory, or fabricated of precious gems and brilliant diamonds.

Whether you make your own or buy them, tassels—like people— have personalities. Some are powerful, some personal, some downright playful. They may be grand and formal or casual and folksy. While all tassels share the aim of adornment, the character of each is different.

Formal tassels might be described as those made by professionals, often with elaborate equipment. In Europe, a five-year apprenticeship was required to become a "passementier"—a maker of trims, cords, braids, and tassels. Most formal tassels are still made by hand and follow a set pattern. These are found

Tasseled Chinese opera stick represents a horse.

in the interior design, fashion, and jewelry industries. Military and graduation tassels fall into this class, as do those found on gourmet menus and wine lists.

Folk tassels, on the other hand, are seldom mass-produced. They are usually handmade by individuals, often for a specific purpose: to decorate an animal, to appease a spirit, or to brighten a corner. Many are made in harsh and humble surroundings and tend to be simple and unique, showing a resourceful use of materials. The possibilities are limited only by the maker's imagination and ingenuity. While folk tassels flourish in the Third World and on native costumes, the lovingly crocheted shade pulls found in the United States belong in the same category.

Whether folk or formal, man's desire for decoration has passed from generation to generation and from culture to culture throughout the centuries . Though never playing more than a minor role, tassels have consistently satisfied this need since the beginning of recorded history.

Left: Carved tassels turn a carousel horse even more joyful.

Bottom right: Chinese opera heroine in the costume of an empress

Tassels Past to Present

Very little has been written about tassels, but the art of earlier times provides silent testimony to their prominence. Evidence of early use can be found in wall paintings, relief carvings, and sculptures. Ancient drawings indicate that clothing was not sewn but wrapped and secured with cords. The warp ends of woven cloth were tied off to prevent raveling, and tassels were formed in the process. Perhaps these tassels, like the proverbial fig leaf, were intended to preserve propriety!

The earliest evidence I have found of actual tassels is on Egyptian royal tomb paintings that display costumes and customs of the day. One painting dated 1900 B.C. depicts a Phoenician prince, draped with tasseled cords, bearing gifts to an Egyptian king. Another, dated 1300 B.C., shows tassels on the corners of royal pillows. Since the purpose of these paintings was to provide for the wants and needs of the deceased as they travelled to the next world, it's impressive that tassels were included!

Centuries ago, in the Middle East, battles and warriors were the themes most often depicted in Assyrian art. Limestone relief carvings and brilliantly colored wall paintings reveal that warriors outfitted their horses with tassels on bridles, saddle pads, and chest plates. These soldiers and their king—with his elaborately tasseled

Top: Neolithic cave painting suggests that tassels may have existed as early as 7000 B.C.

robes—won control of the important trade routes of Western Asia. The tassels probably had nothing to do with the success of the Assyrian conquest, but it is interesting to note that rather than being made of the garment material alone (as in earlier times), these tassels were constructed separately and then attached to clothing or armor.

One of the privileges of rank during ancient times was to be shaded by a tasseled umbrella carried by an attendant or attached to a chariot. Umbrellas weren't commonly used for rain protection until the end of the sixteenth century, yet even when the function changed, the tassels remained.

The Byzantine Empire—established when Emperor Constantine moved the capitol of Rome to Constantinople in A.D. 330—introduced concepts of decoration that affected art throughout Europe for many centuries. Mosaics and manuscripts from the period show that tassels were part of early Christian dress. The church decreed that the body be completely clothed, and the Byzantines, who were fond of luxury (they developed silk making and ivory carving), added adornment wherever possible.

In A.D. 540, Emperor Justinian, with the aid of two Persian monks, managed to smuggle precious and closely guarded silkworm eggs out of China, thereby introducing silk production to the Occidental world and providing a luxury fiber for tassels.

Byzantine man favored tasseled stocking caps. Both he and his lady wore elaborate belts and girdles embellished with tassels made of gold threads and set with jewels. The first fitted clothing appeared during this period, and tassels were a standard accent on most garments.

Between the end of the Byzantine era and the invention of the printing press, hand-written and hand-colored illuminated books provide us with one of the best records

of life in the Middle Ages. Christian monks decorated these manuscripts with elaborate letters and intricate scenes in gold, silver, and vibrant colors. Throughout their magnificent illustrations, tassels are depicted on tents and carriages, canopied thrones and beds, clothing, pillows, and Bible cloths. Tassels also appear in illustrations of monks' robes, suggesting that book design was not the monks' sole artistic endeavor.

During this same period, tassels were also common in the Arab world, as evidenced in the exquisitely illustrated Koran, or Moslem holy book. Tassels are still a part of Arab dress. The agal, or ring, that holds the Arab headcloth commonly has small black tassels, originally made of goat hair, on the cords, and the traditional over-robe, or kibr, is tied with tassels as well.

Bedouin Arab

New Guinea fertility figure

The Moors had a profound influence on Spanish ornamentation. Immense amounts of gold and silver bullion—obtained through the exploits of Spanish navigators—produced an aristocracy whose homes were adorned with silk, velvet, and damask hangings. These wall pieces were appliquéd and trimmed with the most elaborate gold braids, fringes, and tassels. Heavy draperies, canopies, chandeliers, cushions, and small boxes were all embellished with tassels—in traditional Arab fashion—to suit the formal tastes of the wealthy Spaniard.

Formal tassels may have originated in China. According to legend, when the emperor's subjects approached him, they held the silk pendants on their court robes in their hands to assure that their voluminous sleeves concealed no weapons. Chinese women, who considered small feet to be a status symbol, affixed tassels on their skirts and tiny shoes to emphasize the awkward, painful hobble caused by the practice of foot binding. Whatever their function in China, the use of formal tassels quickly spread as trade with Europe increased.

The word "tassel" apparently evolved during the Middle Ages when fashionable ladies wore draped cloaks or mantles fastened at the neck with metal ornaments called "tasseaus" (from the Latin word "tassa," or clasp). Tassel-tipped cords were pulled through these ornaments to close the garment. After the twelfth century, the meaning expanded to include the tassel itself. The word also described a band of cloth, usually black, used to fill plunging décolletages: "Tasseaus" to the rescue!

The poet Geoffrey Chaucer, who is credited with furthering the development of the English language, may have given us literature's first mention of tassels in *The Canterbury Tales*:

"And by hire girdel heng a purs of lether,
 Tasseled with greene and perled with latoun."

Unlike many of the words in this passage, "tasseled" has at least retained its original spelling. Leaping from Chaucer to the jungle, we read in Malcolm Kirk's book *Man As Art: New Guinea* that today the word "tasol" is Pidgin English for decoration. And these tribes do indeed use tassels as "tasol"!

While women were securing their mantles with tassels, men were using them to keep their pants up. Early leg coverings consisted of cloth wrapped around the calf and tied under the knee with a cord and a tassel. As breeches grew shorter, the hose became longer, but until hose were finally joined at the crotch (to form tights), the tasseled garter was an indispensable accessory.

The embroidered Bayeux tapestry shows Norman

noblemen with the fringe on their hose tied to the side, forming tassels. This custom survives today. African soldiers use a tasseled garter to hold up their socks. The Greek fustanella (akin to the Scottish kilt) is worn with a tasseled cap and tasseled garters. Bavarians have kept the tassel, moving it from their socks to their liederhosen, where it no longer serves as a garter but does carry on the tradition.

Damsels in the Middle Ages wore garters just as men did—silk and velvet ones embroidered with gold thread and embellished with jewels and tassels. While no pious nun of the time would have displayed her garters, I noticed in a fourteenth century brass engraving that tassels dangled from the sacred bag in which one devout nun carried her prayer book.

Flemish artist Jan van Eyck, a master of detail, included tassels in his famous painting *Arnolfini and His Bride*. (Look for these on the wall depicted in the painting, under the artist's signature.) And no, the bride in this work isn't pregnant. She just needs a tasseled cord to hold up her voluminous skirt.

After the printing press was invented, text was produced mechanically, but illustrations were still hand-carved in wood and block-printed. The artist and technical craftsman Albrecht Durer—one of the first artists to sign his own work—was a master of this technique. Note the intricately carved, elaborate valence of tassels in his *Birth Bed of the Virgin*.

The era of castles, kings, and elegant trappings provided numerous opportunities for European tassel and trim makers. In 1559 the French formed a guild for the express purpose of producing "passementerie". Tools, equipment, skilled workers, and apprentices were assembled to produce tassels for all who could afford them.

The French, who perfected the tassel and recorded its history, continue to recognize this art form. In 1973 the Paris Musée des Arts honored tassel and trim makers in a show that documented each period from the Renaissance to Art Nouveau and described the shape, size, type, and fabric color of French tassels. While designs and materials change, the decorative function of tassels remains the same.

Henry VIII's court painter, Hans Holbein (the younger),

recorded sixteenth century costumes and decorations, providing a visual record of tassels on clothing and in interiors. (Six wives require a lot of tassels!) Holbein painted grand salons with drapes and chairs adorned to complement the tasseled cloaks, hats, girdles, and purses of men and women alike. Purses were miniature works of art,

La Passementière

covered with embroidery, stump-work, beading, or silk- and metal-thread canvas work. The drawstrings and edges of these bags were lavishly enriched with silk and metal tassels.

Purses became obsolete for men during the early seventeenth century, when pockets were added to men's pants. Even so, tassels remained in the male wardrobe. Leather game bags and falconers' gloves with straps and tassels completed the sporting Englishman's hawking attire, while embroidered and tasseled gauntlets were "de rigueur" among cavaliers. Today, a tassel still hangs from the falconer's glove for no purpose except decoration.

Peter Paul Rubens, the seventeenth century baroque painter whose queen-sized figures gave us the term "Rubenesque," traveled widely as an ambassador, observing courts throughout Europe and documenting nobility, nudes, and tassels in his work.

During this period, starched and wired Elizabethan collars were replaced by looser ones fastened with cords and elaborate lace tassels. Similar collars appear in Colonial American portraits.

The sumptuous style of King Louis XIV in his palace at Versailles is well recorded. There, an influx of Chinese art combined with Italian, French, and Spanish grandeur to inspire overwhelmingly extravagant tassels. In a manner befitting a king, the four posts of Louis's state bed were decorated not only with textile tassels but also with carved wooden tassels. The latter were embellished with large bouquets of ostrich and heron feathers mingled with gold and silver flowers. Considered a symbol of wealth, such ornate beds were not necessarily used for sleeping but often served as the centerpiece of the reception room, where they sported the most elaborate decorations one could afford. Draft protection was provided by heavy

French tassels, XVI-XIX century

curtains held open with tasseled ropes. Later, headboards were draped with great fabric swags fastened in place with cords and tassels. The whole bed resembled one huge pile of cloth and tassels, or as one writer of the day described it, "hyperboles of velvet."

Briefly, during the mid-seventeenth century, "excessive decoration in dress and accessories" was banned, and tassels became less common. However, in the eighteenth and nineteenth centuries tassels burgeoned and appeared on gentlemen's watch fobs, waistcoats, and gloves, and on women's gowns and accessories.

Marie Antoinette must have considered tassels as important as cake. While she frittered away the French monarchy, the embellishment of her gowns and her Petit Trianon chateau commanded the finest of the French tassel maker's art. These tassels were not restricted to

An antique French tassel

fabrics. Tassel-inspired designs were carved in wood, cast in metal, and printed on wallpaper. Intricate bronze mounts, beaded robes, swags, and festoons of tassels were added to inlaid and carved furniture.

After the guillotine severed the French monarchy, tassels became a patriot's emblem. Revolutionary flags

The author's grandmother tasseled out for some splendid occasion

and furniture, murals and textiles, generals and battlements were blanketed with tassels. Many craft guilds were abolished during the Revolution; the Reign of Terror and the Napoleonic Wars further impoverished society. Nevertheless, Emperor Napoleon I demanded furnishings and clothing consistent with his ego. The Louvre and his other apartments were flamboyantly decorated with tassels; his uniforms were lavishly covered with gold tassels.

Empress Josephine also had a flair for tassels. While Napoleon was busy building an empire, she borrowed extravagantly to purchase her own domicile, Malmaison. She hired Charles Percier and Pierre Fontain—the men who gave birth to the concept of "interior decorators"—to create an imperial style complete with indoor tents and tasseled flagpoles. A body-conscious woman, Josephine was known to wet her gowns until they clung to her perfectly. Though tassels enhanced the provocative effect, they failed to aid Josephine in her efforts to produce an heir, so Napoleon took a second wife, Marie Louise, who did conceive a son—perhaps with the help of her bed. Described as "less a piece of furniture than a monument," it boasted life-sized carved figures and gold-and-white curtains tied with tassels and topped with ostrich plumes. History doesn't reveal whether any tassels were exiled with Napoleon to Elbe or to St. Helena, but we do know that neither of his wives was allowed to go. Josephine remained in Malmaison, while Marie Louise and Napoleon II lived in tasseled grandeur in Vienna.

During the Victorian era, trade and industry flourished, creating a middle class eager for adornment. The Industrial Revolution advanced the technology of luxury arts, replacing exclusive hand craftsmanship with mechanical mass production and allowing many to have what was once available only to the wealthy. The United States lacked kings and courts, but Victorian fashion provided ample opportunity for displaying tassels on draperies, gowns, horses, and carriages. A myriad of objects and places were ripe for embellishment.

Fashion books in the 1860s featured tassels on women's capes, hoods, and high-top shoes, and as the century progressed, so did the use of tassels. Scarves, sashes, parasols, and gloves were all adorned. Parasols became a popular fashion item when the invention of steel ribs allowed them to be made lighter than earlier models (making shade-bearing attendants unnecessary). Tassels brightened the edges and handle cords, producing a dainty and feminine accessory.

By the turn of the century, trims and tassels epitomized the genteel life. Not only were interiors heavily fringed, but clothes were as well. A photograph of Edwardian high society at Ascot in 1910 shows women in mourning for King Edward VII dressed completely in black: black dresses, black feathered hats, and (of course) black tassels. In contrast to earlier times, men's fashions had become more tailored and subdued. Tassels continued to appear on women's clothing, however, and interiors sparkled with chandeliers, mirrors, paintings, and portraits all hung with elegant, tasseled ropes.

In the early 1900s, designer Paul Poiret burst onto the Paris fashion scene, declaring that women's figures looked like "a pair of semi-circles towing a barge and should be liberated." This he accomplished by banishing the corset and inventing the brassiere, thus revolutionizing women's fashion. His loose and fluid robes were designed with elegant, tasseled cords, which he justified as "something for the lady to play with."

Poiret was the first courtier to show his collection across Europe. While in Russia, he met a young man named Romain de Tiroff, who later became his assistant designer and who greatly influenced the use and style of tassels.

Tiroff descended from a long line of military heroes and was not sure how his chosen profession of "clothing designer" would be received by his family. To avoid any embarrassment, he combined his initials, "R" and "T" (pronouncing them "Erté") and used this name throughout his long and productive career. When Poiret closed his business, Erté ventured out on his own and turned his talents to the American fashion scene.

Wealthy publisher William Randolph Hearst hired Erté to design covers for *Harper's Bazaar*, which Erté did for twenty-two years, creating during that time—and for fifty more years—many fanciful tassels designed to be used lavishly on clothing, jewelry, and accessories as well as furniture, interiors, theater costumes, and film sets. Erté's sketches illustrate the most original and imaginative places for tassels. He used exuberant and luxurious materials such as ermine skins, ostrich feathers, silk, and jewels.

World War I brought about the demise of the French couturier, as the fine laces and embroidery of the Edwardian era were set aside during the war effort. Society women, accustomed to such finery, turned to nursing and charity work, and their servants entered factories. Convenience and comfort were required in the clothing of all classes; the extensive use of tassels languished.

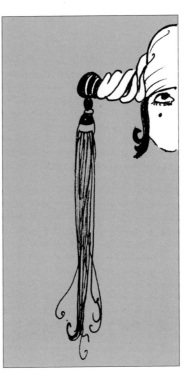

Erté-style sketches

After the war, many women remained in the work force and became—along with their clothing—less restricted. As prosperity returned, dancing and sports became popular. Fashion followed function, and as always, tassels followed fashion. Dance dresses were short, shapeless, and covered with beads, sequins, and tassels. Links of fine wire formed into tassels materialized on purses. Beaded tassels dangled from flappers' necks and ears, and tasseled floor lamps and shades added a frivolous touch that matched the times.

Movies and music halls featured the showy costumes of entertainers like the Dolly Sisters and Mae West, and tassels were well represented. Many a burlesque dancer might have landed in jail were it not for those discreetly

placed decorations. Rudolph Valentino—one of the most expensively dressed stars of the 1920s—appeared in tassel-trimmed outfits. Theaters were lavishly festooned with plush drapes, velour curtains, and dazzling tassels.

The austere 1930s and 1940s generated little in the way of ornamentation. Tassels were relegated to ceremonial functions, film sets, and theatrical costumes. (Vivian Leigh's green velvet drapery ensemble in *Gone With the Wind* was fitted to her figure with yellow tasseled cords.)

After World War II, our tastes embraced the "new and modern." Mass production became a way of life, and in so-called civilized cultures, the fanciful tassel temporarily fell victim to industrialization.

Tassels were by no means extinct, however. They flourished, as they had for centuries, in all those "uncivilized" cultures—the ones that were not dropping bombs, dividing nations, or inventing other "useful" things. Nomads, tribesmen, farmers, peasants, and other ordinary people continued to craft the superfluous tassel for their own needs. Ironically, while jeans and T-shirts were replacing traditional costumes in remote areas, American peace workers and hippies of the 1960s were collecting and wearing items from these cultures. Afghan, African, Asian, and Arabian folk tassels—many totally unlike any previously seen in the United States—were suddenly available in import and "counter culture" shops.

Folk tassels are as important in their native surroundings as formal tassels are in more sophisticated societies.

The animal hair tassels of Nigerian chiefs proclaim the same authority as the silk and gold tassels of Queen Elizabeth; a nomad's wealth, displayed in tasseled silver jewelry, signifies status as effectively as a diamond-encrusted tassel brooch.

Opposite page: Tassel shop in Katmandu

Top: Looped tassels of sago palm represent food for Asmat tribesmen in Irian Jaya.

Left: Hammered silver tassels from Afghanistan

Unlike their formal counterparts, folk tassels are fashioned from whatever materials are available. Their makers must rely on creativity and resourcefulness rather than on the store around the corner and the factory down the road.

I have seen tassels made from almost every conceivable animal, vegetable, and mineral: hair from elephants, horses, humans, and totally unrecognizable sources; furs from ermine, mink, squirrel, and possum; feathers from chickens, ostriches, marabou, and exotic birds of the Amazon (sometimes with beaks and heads included); animal tails, shells, coins, buttons, crepe paper, thimbles, bullets, tin-can pieces, leather (often with hair attached), rags, plastic, and amazing combinations of these. (I have one tassel made from silkworm cocoons!) Hanks of grass, stalks of grain, and palm fronds are pressed into service. After all, when you need a tassel, sticks, stones, and bones may be the only materials available!

In nearly all cultures and climates, native costumes are enlivened with tassels. Bits of metal, pieces of yarn, and clusters of feathers jangle and sway from hats and shoes, elbows and ankles. In the Arctic, Eskimos design tassels from strips of hide to decorate dog sleds and parkas. In

Ladakh dowry piece

Native Americans put horsehair to elegant use in these tassels.

the Black Forest of Germany, red pompons on a woman's hat announce that she's single; in parts of India, a red tassel twined in the hair indicates the same status. Black tassels are worn by widows in Nepal. In Mexico, men wear tiny tassels on their hats and women braid them in their hair.

Throughout the world, tassels proclaim celebration and joy. Almost all folk dancers will use tassels somewhere to accentuate their movements. And can you imagine bag-

pipes or pipers without tassels? For that matter, the mystery of what a Scotsman wears under his kilt might be revealed if not for the tasseled sporran!

Neither are animals forgotten in the world of tassels. From the Rose Bowl to Main Street on the Fourth of July, no parade would be complete without at least a few tasseled animals. And how about those 1950s pompon-clipped French poodles? They were a bit of folk art all by themselves. At funerals in Indonesia, sacrificial water buffalo are adorned with tassels for presentation to the deceased. Basque herders employ a tasseled covering to protect the eyes of their oxen from flies. A camel's great height allows for long, flowing tassels to be suspended from its neck, chest, and chin. Yaks on the Tibetan tundra, water buffalo in Asian rice paddies, llamas in the Peruvian highlands, camels, elephants, horses, and other beasts of burden are decked out with tassels each morning to perform their unending labors.

Even Mother Nature creates her own tassels: on trees, shrubs, flowers, and grasses, not to mention tasseled birds, tasseled fish, and even tasseled crabs. The weaver bird of Thailand forms a cozy tassel nest in which to raise her young. And without the pollen from a tassel, there would be no corn.

As for more formal tassels, some experts feel that the interior design world of the 1990s will resurrect the opulence of the 1880s. As noted designer, Mario Buatta, puts it, "All I see are people reaching into the past to feather their nests." If the deluge of new fashion catalogues I've received myself is any indication, those feathers may well be tassels; in one, a model wears an elegant suit with gold-

Red tassels on this yak brighten a bleak Tibetan winter.

Ear tassels identify llamas in the Andes

cord trim, and eight large, black tassels are visible on the jacket. (Who knows how many are in back!) She's also wearing long, gold tassel earrings. In another, a lipstick ad features a woman wearing even longer rayon tassels in a shade that matches the lip color. In the more exclusive catalogues, diamonds, gemstones, tassel pins, pendants, and earrings abound. Black patterned stockings sporting tiny tassels down the back seam can be ordered to wear with velvet shoes that have gold-braided tassel designs on the instep. For a sportier look, the familiar tassel loafer is readily available for all ages and sexes.

If actual tassels—whether hard or soft—aren't enough, you can order a tassel-print skirt with matching scarf. These should be worn when you serve dinner in your tasseled dining room—be sure the chair cushions, rug corners, picture hangers, drapes, and window shades are all tasseled to complement your outfit. Wear your hair in a pony-tail tassel or braided into beaded cornrow tassels. If you aren't serving too many guests, use the pedestal table offered by one catalogue; it's carved in the shape of a tassel. Gold-tasseled napkin rings complete the look, and if it's a Christmas party, the tree can be trimmed with assorted tassel ornaments.

There are all sorts of tassels to suit all sorts of people all over the world. From cave paintings to current catalogues, tassels wind through time and weave through cultures. They are a continuous weft in the warp of centuries—a weft of pure pleasure and delicious delight. And their appeal—the appeal of fun regardless of function—is universal.

Power Tassels

Perhaps because tassels appeared on garments very early in our history, they assumed a symbolic significance. Some signify authority. They demand attention. They imply special powers, or they impart stature to the bearer. Whether their potency results from myth, magic, or religious ritual, these tassels assert a power of command over an audience. The sticks and staffs of kings, priests, and healers are made more powerful with the addition of tassels. The heraldry of both church and state uses them to denote rank and authority. Tassels have a place in military attire and in pomp and ceremony. They are also used as offerings to spirits, both good and evil.

At graduation ceremonies, many of us have had the experience of moving a tassel from one side of a mortarboard to the other. For that moment, with this simple act, we felt a sense of accomplishment and importance. And any of you who were honors students may have worn a tasseled rope over your shoulders to show your exceptional achievement.

The graduation cap dates to antiquity. The English poet George Gascoigne, writing in 1456, says it was given by God himself to the doctors of Mosaic Law. He adds that since the days of King Alfred only doctors of divinity and canon law were allowed to wear this badge of rank.

Under Roman law, slaves were freed by being allowed to wear a cap. The academic community later

An Asmat dagger is created from the shinbone of a cassowary bird. The tassels are made with the bird's feathers and with local seeds. (Irian Jaya)

Bottom: Dignitaries displayed their status with these badges during the 1920s. Gold bullion tassels trim the rosettes.

Top center: Graduation tassel

Top right: Catholic priest (Mexico)

adopted the cap as a symbol of independence for those with masters and doctor of divinity degrees. Originally it was round, soft, and draped gracefully from a center tuft or pompon. Seventeenth century portraits of clergymen, like Vandyke's *Archbishop Land*, illustrate this style.

After the Reformation, bachelors of arts and undergraduates were allowed to wear the cap as well, and the tuft was replaced by a tassel. Once this coveted badge of medieval authority was extended, the tassel became a symbol of rank. Gold tassels were reserved for peers and their eldest sons.

Tassels are also a designation of rank in the ecclesiastical world. The Roman Catholic origins of this tradition date from the thirteenth century, when Pope Innocent IV decreed that a red hat with matching tassels would be a sign of authority for cardinals. This flat, wide-brimmed hat was worn at both church and state functions and was a symbol of ecclesiastical power even after its wearer's death. In Notre Dame

Cardinals await Pope John Paul II.
(Prague, Czechoslovakia)

Cathedral, red-corded tasseled hats hang from the 115-foot ceiling over the tombs of cardinals buried below.

At the Council of Lyons in 1248, the tasseled hat was adopted as a heraldic crest for all Catholic clergy. The number of tassels allocated to each rank has varied through the years, but in 1832 a standard was established. Cardinals receive fifteen tassels on each side. Archbishops use a green hat with ten tassels to a side. Bishops are entitled to six tassels, while priests, canons, and vicars rate a black hat flanked by a single tassel on each side. Red and violet tassels signify other positions in the Catholic church.

Tassels are used as symbols on the coats of arms of individual clergy, where they may appear on crests and seals or embroidered on stoles. The Pope's official insignia consists of a tiara and two keys interlaced with a tasseled cord. Throughout the Vatican, tassels are carved on walls and doors, draped on canopies, and depicted in paintings.

The coat of arms of the Church of England's Cardinal Wolsey displays tassels. Scottish clergy don black hats with black tassels, except for the queen's chaplain, who rates red tassels and cords. The dean of the Royal Chapel merits three red tassels on his hat.

Crests and insignia are not the only emblems of

ecclesiastical rank upon which tassels appear. Religious vestments are often embellished with them, as are stoles and cinctures, the hoods of copes, and altar linens of many faiths.

The Bible makes several references to tassels. In Num. 15:39-40, the Lord tells Moses that the Israelites should wear tassels on the borders of their garments as a reminder to curb unruly desires and to obey God's commandments. In some translations, tassel size is designated as at least the length of three fingers. Deut. 22:12 states that tassels should be placed on the four corners of one's outer garment.

In the New Testament, Mark 6:56, we are told that those who touched the tassels on Jesus' cloak were cured of their illnesses. Luke 8:44 states that a sick woman who touched Jesus' tasseled hem was likewise healed. In Matt. 23:5, Jesus rebukes the scribes and Pharisees for wearing tassels which are too long.

Tassels are still worn in the Jewish religion, just as Moses prescribed. During one early period when Jews were persecuted, the tassels were moved to undergarments. Now, they are to be worn only when they can be seen, which is usually interpreted to mean during natural daylight. Hence they are used mainly at morning prayer.

Married men in Orthodox synagogues and all men in Conservative and Reform Jewish synagogues wear a prayer shawl (tallit) with tassels (tzitzit) on the corners. The tassels transform the shawl into a tallit and represent recognition of the commandments in the four corners of the earth. When the tallit is donned, the tassels are gathered and held around one finger, and each is kissed during prayer. Jewish boys (and now some girls) receive their first tallit when they are recognized as adults at a Bar (or Bat) Mitzvah ceremony. The tassels may be made of wool, linen, or silk but must not be of mixed fiber, just as—according to Orthodox Law—meat and milk may not be eaten together.

Forming the tzitzit requires a ritual sequence, which starts with a granny knot. Traditionally the ends are bitten rather than cut. The tassel's wrapping represents "bringing together" and signifies that "God is one." Eight strands and five knots are tied in a manner that represent the 613 commandments in the Torah. Tzitzit kits are available at Hebrew book stores.

When a Jewish man dies, he may be buried in the shawl, but one of the tassels must be removed so that the shawl is no longer a tallit. At Jewish weddings, the tallit may be used as a chupa (or canopy). The chupa repre-

Muslim prayer beads (Ethiopia)

Buddhist practices vary greatly. In Thailand and Tibet, males—some as young as six years old—don orange robes, shave their heads, and serve as monks. During their service, which lasts at least six months, they refrain from meat, women, and alcohol, but tassels are never forbidden.

Tibetan Buddhist monks employ special daggers during exorcism rituals, the sheaths of which are inlaid with coral, turquoise, and silver and trimmed with knotted silk tassels. Brightly painted monastery doors feature a center brass medallion with a cloth tassel and

Figure of Kobo Dai Shi Kukai, founder of a small Buddhist sect, fingering his tasseled prayer beads. Such figures are placed in shrines.

sents a home; it may consist of a floral bower, tassel-decorated covering, or tallit (as long as one can see the stars).

In the Greek Orthodox church, the empty tomb of Christ is represented by a structure called the Epitaphio; its roof is trimmed with carved wooden tassels. The Epitaphio rests on the right-hand side of the altar for most of the year, but during a ceremony on Holy Friday evening, it is carried around the church along with lighted candles. Tassels are used on vestments and altar cloths, and priests wear a stole with rows of tassels or fringe on the bottom to represent the added weight and responsibility they have in caring for the souls in their charge.

Tassels play an important role in Eastern religions as well. Moslems and Hindus use tassels on their religious beads and counters, and Buddhists tie their meditation beads together with a tassel. (The Buddhist word for tassel is "sutra," from the Sanskrit word that means to unite or bring together. Like the wrapping on the tzitzit, this use of tassels can serve as a meaningful symbol for us all.) Tassels appear on crowns, spangles, and necklaces in early paintings of Buddha; they continue to be used as offerings and as decorations on statues of him.

tubular woven tassels to the sides. Dark interiors are dimly lit by pungent yak-oil lamps; the grimy walls are thick with yak grease left from pilgrims' hands. Monks sit on their pallets fingering tasseled beads, while silk-pieced cloth tassels flutter overhead. These large, three-dimensional tassel forms hang from ceilings and columns or sway on poles outdoors. Appliquéd and embroidered symbols crown their tops. Himalayan prayer flags soon become shredded, but the tattered tassels continue to lift prayers to heaven.

Hinduism originated in India over four thousand years ago. Followers believe that souls are reincarnated until they can be reunited with Brahman, the supreme spirit. There are hundreds of tassel-adorned gods to help the soul achieve this final goal. Tassel-decorated shells serve as trumpets and as water containers during auspicious occasions in both Hindu and Buddhist ceremonies.

Left: Monastery door (Tibet)

Below: Prayer flags (Tibet)

Top left: Worry beads from Greece and Buddhist prayer counter from Nepal

Top right: Straw tassels protect venerated trees from cold and snow. (Japan)

Bottom right: Traditional Oshogatsu New Year's decorations. Large straw tassels are hung outside the front door; smaller straw and paper ones are placed on the Shinto altar inside.

Although worry beads have no religious significance, people of the Middle East, Greece, and Turkey often carry them—with a tassel attached—to release tension. When negotiations get tough, beads and tassels may appear.

In the Middle East, evil spirits are believed to fear fringes, so tassels are good protection. Tassels serve a similar purpose in the Shinto religion. Priests hang shimenawa (twisted straw ropes with white paper or straw tassels) in front of shrines to protect them and to mark the boundary between sacred and unholy places. These tassels must always be twisted to the left to drive out evil. During the New Year, tassels are hung in front of houses to assure good fortune.

Shintoists honor the gods of nature, teach a joyful attitude toward life, and emphasize the need to adapt to one's environment, whether one is dealing with plants or skyscrapers. Old and venerated trees are sheltered from the cold and snow with straw tassels. Tassels made of white paper and parts of the nusa plant are waved to appease Shinto deities during ceremonies in church on the Sabbath but are also used whenever a house, car, or factory undergoes ritual purification.

The belief that some persons can influence good and evil is widespread; from American Indians to Australian aborgines and from Africa to Asia, tassels

Shaman's shirt (Mali)

are used to help control the spirits that inhabit the shaman's world. The rituals and costumes vary, but more often than not the elaborate mystical regalia includes tassels.

Essential to a shaman's coat are the various pendants used to attract guardian spirits or to protect against evil ones. Spirits appear in dreams and instruct the shaman, and their ritual demands must be closely followed. The shaman shakes when evil spirits are sensed, so tassels and other appendages contain metal to create enough noise to ensure the spirits' hurried departure. Each special object in the shaman's arsenal, including the tassel—a symbol of terror and power—helps to maintain control over the spirit world.

A glance at Native American art illustrates that the tassel has long been a traditional element in rituals and ceremonies. One shaman's mask from the Pacific Northwest sports a wolf's head, a human skull, and long, red cloth tassels. Ojibwa medicine men designed tassels from polished deer hooves to rattle over their patients. Plains Indians carried magic herbs and other paraphernalia in an otter's body; its feet and tail were replaced by quill or bead work, and its toes were represented by metal-cone tassels stuffed with hair. Cheyenne and Arapaho sacred quill-makers used a holy embroidery to embellish beaded and deer-toe tassels on a baby's cradle; the tassels represented parts of the body and served as tokens for long life and good health.

Shaman's stick (Africa)

Many an Indian chief proclaimed his authority with a long, feathered, and tasseled headdress, and additional status was given to tomahawks, war clubs, and pipes by decorating them with hide, hair, feather, and cloth tassels. Blackfoot Indians brandished leather-covered, stone war-clubs—adorned with fierce beaded faces and feather tassels—to terrify their enemies in hand-to-hand combat. The Sioux used tassels consisting of metal cones with feather or hair suspensions as decorations. Plains Indians showed off their victims' scalps by embellishing each scalp with beads, braiding the hair below it, and hanging beadwork tassels from the braided locks; the whole object—beaded scalp and dangling hair—resembled one elegant tassel.

Among some Arctic tribes, the glance of a young girl was thought to be so powerful that it could render a hunter incapable of hitting game. To prevent such an occurrence and to assure that the village would

not go hungry, pubescent females were required to wear beaded and tasseled veils.

Other cultures employed tassels to assure a plentiful food supply; the tassel corn dolls used in Western grain regions provide just one example. Early farmers believed that the spirit of the harvest lived in grain and controlled the growth of crops. Each year at harvest time, the last stalks were gathered and plaited to form a winter resting place for this spirit. The bundle was placed in the home or church for safekeeping. In the spring, the cycle began anew when seeds from the previous year's bundle were mixed with new grains for a propitious harvest.

In Torajaland, where rice is the major crop, a woman goes alone to the field before the harvest begins and knots seven stalks to make a tassel, thus

Below and opposite page: Native American shaman paraphernalia

binding the soul of the rice to the ground so that it can't escape during cutting.

In parts of India and Africa, where women are the water carriers, a head ring is often worn to help balance the container. To protect the precious load, cowrie-shell tassels (symbols of fertility and wealth) and yarn tassels (symbols of the need for rain) are attached to the ring. To repel evil spirits that might spill or infect the water, shisha mirrors are also added.

Every year in May, Thai farm animals are decorated with tassels and paraded in front of the Grand Palace during the Royal Ploughing ceremony to assure the success of the coming year's crop.

Human beings are greatly outnumbered by all manner of spirits in Thailand. Every home, village, city, factory, or bend in the road seems to have a spirit house where a benevolent soul can take up residence and keep mischievous spirits away. The architectural motif on the roofs of these structures is called a chofa, or sky tassel, and is the last piece to be added. Its purpose is to allow spirits to keep in contact with each other.

Carved forms along the roof of this Thai spirit house are called sky tassels.

Floral tassel offerings (Thailand)

Thai astral beings must be placated with offerings ranging from sweets to jugs of wine. Each entity has its favorite; one roadside curve is protected by a female spirit who likes carved wooden phallic figures. Colorful tassels of plastic and spent silkworm cocoons make suitable offerings too. Floral tassel offerings, however, are appreciated by all. Fabricating these keeps people busy from morning to night stringing sweet-smelling buds, jasmine, and orchids into tassels and tying them with ribbons. The fragrant results are presented not only to spirits, but to Buddha at temples (wats in the Thai language), altars, and statues as well.

Bali is another place full of spirits, temples, and tassels. In this magic land, tassels in the sky serve as a bridge between heaven and earth, and tasseled stone figures stand guard outside buildings. During the festive holiday of Galungan, celebrated once every 210 days, each village is decorated in much the same way as we decorate at Christmas. The streets are lined with bamboo poles covered with tassels (called lamak) made from

Opposite page: In Bali, tassels serve as a bridge between heaven and earth.

Festive Galungan tassels (Bali)

finely cut coconut palm, banana, and papyrus leaves; marigolds are added for color. Days go into the crafting of these as each family creates elaborate, colorful, and intricately cut designs. The skies are alive with the ripple and rustle of these tassels, while shrines and offering platforms are completely bedecked with them.

In other parts of the world, the skies bloom with kites during certain festivals. Kites provide a way to reach the rain gods and to assure a good harvest. The Chinese construct a fertility kite by tying unthreshed rice into tassels and attaching them to the kite's sides and tail. When the kite is flown over a new rice field, the wind shakes the grain from the straw. If the kite stays aloft until all the seeds have dropped, the farmer is henceforth assured of a plentiful crop from this field.

During the Day of the Dead festivities in Guatemala, enormous kites are flown—some as large as seventeen feet in diameter—with tassels fluttering around their entire perimeters. This Mayan custom developed as a way of sending messages to ancestors and departed loved ones.

The sharp sound of air striking the paper tassels on the giant kites of Santiago, Guatemala, is believed to frighten even the bravest of evil apparitions. Today, what began as a witch doctor's ritual has evolved into an annual competition. Each huge flying spectacle is judged on the basis of size, design, and length of time in the air and is flown for three days. Those that survive are finally burned.

Kite flying is serious business in Korea, China, and Japan. Originally performed for religious purposes, kite flying has only recently become a sport. Over the years, tassels have been added to Oriental kites for aerodynamic as well as for decorative and religious purposes.

Pink tassels on a Chinese kite symbolize approaching success, but tassels serve a more immediate function on the famed fighting kites of Nagasaki, Japan. Each of the latter kites (called hata) is equipped with a dangling, twenty-foot line that has been covered with a paste of ground glass. The line is maneuvered to saw through an opponent's kite string and cut the kite loose. Paper tassels maintain balance on the kites' sides as the battle ensues; they are trimmed to assure precision and to counteract any absorption of moisture.

Many tribes use tassels as power symbols. The Asmat men of Irian Jaya—master carvers known for their ceremonial ancestor poles, dugout war canoes, and shields—imbue sacred artifacts with even greater power and protective qualities by embellishing them with tassels made from grass, feathers, or palms. They split sago palm leaves and roll them on their thighs to form tassels, which are then attached to the sides of their phallic war shields. Asmat daggers are carved from the shinbone of a cassowary bird and are decorated with tassels made from the feathers. The same style of tassel is utilized on both men's and women's headbands. Cassowaries are large, aggressive, flightless birds that are difficult to catch; perhaps the feathered tassels are worn to capture some of these qualities.

New Guinea tribes add tassels made of dyed pandanas fibers to carved fertility figures. Tassels decorate yam masks and cover the entire body in dance ceremonies. Members of the Huli group from the island's southern highlands wear woven loin aprons fringed with pigtail tassels. The Asaro tribe decorates its cult houses with magical objects: chains, feathers, and tassels. The Sepik River region has many fine carvers who trim their masks with tassels made from human and animal hair, feathers, and shells; boars' tusks may be added.

Beaded tassels mixed with bird skulls were attached to the sword scabbards of the Dayak tribe in Borneo, where beadwork is a male activity. The Nagas of India put goat-hair and plant-fiber tassels on their hide warshields. Lois Sherr Dubin, in *The History of Beads*, says that dyed goat hair "symbolizes the flames that have ravaged enemy villages." She is referring to a beaded

Fertility figure (New Guinea)

Headhunters of Sarawak, Borneo, added tassels to show how many of their enemies' heads they had claimed.

sash worn across the chest that terminates in three colorful metal and goat-hair tassels.

The Secoyas Indians, who have inhabited the rain forests of Peru for five hundred years, create armband tassels from a fragrant bark.

The headhunters of Sarawak, Borneo added tassels to the tips of their swords each time they took an enemy's head. This attachment, known as a "tali sentagai," was worn only by the bravest warriors. Nowadays the adornment is worn during the ritual festivals of Gawai Burong.

Below: Tassels suspended from the waist represent what once would have been heads of slain enemies. (Flores Island, Indonesia)

Opposite page: Flowing plant-fiber tassels aid an Indonesian firewalker.

Southeast of Borneo, on the Indonesian island of Flores, heavily tattooed men, wearing tassels on their belts to represent what once would have been the heads of their enemies, perform a ceremonial war dance. Music is provided by tapping together long bamboo poles held close to the ground; older women, regarded as invaluable treasures, dance in and out of these poles in time to the beat. In other parts of Indonesia, the practice of walking barefoot through fire is aided by huge plant-fiber tassels.

The customs and beliefs of the Torajan people have not changed for centuries. These residents of the Indonesian island, Sulawesi, believe that they have descended from a hole in the sky and are only on this earth to reach their final resting place in the stars. Death is therefore a joyous occasion, and most of one's life is spent amassing enough funds to afford an appropriate funeral. The deceased is left in his or her home until the family can furnish a suitable send-off. Then, friends and relatives assemble for a week's celebration. Four-foot-long, beaded circular tassels are typical decorations. Temporary bamboo shelters are built to accommodate the guests, who arrive with offerings ranging from cigarettes to pigs. Water buffalo are the most prized offering—spotted ones raised expressly for this purpose are the most valuable gift of all—and are decorated with elaborate, colorful tasseled headpieces. Gifts are accounted for, and repayment in kind is expected at the donor's funeral. (Consequently one village owes me a small pig!)

Top: Sacrificial water buffalo (Torajaland)

Bottom: Initiation and circumcision mask (Mali)

On the fourth day of the funeral, the animals are slaughtered; their souls accompany the deceased, and their meat is used to feed the guests. Very practical.

Circumcision masks are used in a number of African cultures. During initiation ceremonies in Mali, when young males are instructed in the ways of the tribe and older men pass from one level to the next, participants wear carved wooden masks with a repousse metal overlay decorated with red yarn tassels. Similar but much smaller versions are used as "passports" when their wearers go from one region to another.

There is a belief in some areas of Pakistan that if a witch can cut a pregnant woman's hair and bundle it into a tassel, the woman's baby will be stillborn; jealous mothers-in-law practice this custom.

Can you imagine a parade of soldiers, the roll of drums, the blare of trumpets, and the cadence of marching feet without the sheen and glitter of gold tassels? Battle—a recurrent theme since men decided that war was a means to power—always seems to include more elaborate trappings than those of peace. Since early times, tassels have gone to war. The bow and arrow was one of the earliest weapons, and archers frequently hung tassels from their belts to wipe their arrows. The Assyrians flaunted tassels in battle as have numerous armies since.

Prior to the arrival of Buddhism in Japan, it was customary to bury a Japanese soldier with his armor. Emperor Shomu (A.D. 724-48) built a warehouse to

Opposite: World War I poster

Bottom left: Chinese soldier's costume (Tibet)

Bottom right: Figure of Japanese soldier and horse (courtesy of Arms and Armour Press)

preserve the arts, crafts, and weapons of his time. Much was preserved, giving historians a valuable glimpse into early Japanese culture.

Japanese armor was designed to terrify the enemy as well as to protect the warrior; perhaps the flowing silk tassels flapping from both horse and rider were worn to enhance these tactics. Made in sections, these protective coverings were laced with woven silk braids. Because many fine strands of silk were used in the braids, bushy tassels resulted when the ends were tied off. The same braids were used to secure the helmet under the chin. Some helmets had a hole in the top through which the warrior's topknot of hair passed, giving the appearance of another tassel. Silk braids with long tassels were also used on horses' tack.

By 1192 the samurai ruled Japan. These warriors came from the aristocracy and appreciated fine things, including armor that was as handsome and aesthetically pleasing as possible. When a samurai went to war, his armor was packed in a special box tied with tasseled cords. Commanders brandished batons with long hair tassels; the hair was later replaced by paper tassels. And the emperor of Japan's crown was tied with a tasseled cord.

Top right: Japanese helmet with topknot tassel

Bottom right: Japanese warrior hat (Muromachi period, circa 1500)

Top left: In Japan, Boy's Day festivities include samurai warrior dolls.

Top right: Greek soldier

Bottom right: Bagpipes

The samurai era is remembered each year on May 5th during the Boy's Day festival. For one month, Japanese boys eat "soldier food," honor the heroics of their ancestors, and display dolls dressed as famous warriors. These dolls, usually given to youths at their birth by a grandparent, illustrate how elaborate the clothing and tassels of these early warriors were.

Throughout Europe, officers with tasseled swords, hats, and horses led their various armies in parades while honor guards bearing tasseled banners marched ahead to the tune of tasseled trumpets. Since their founding in 1503, the Pope's Swiss guards have embellished their uniforms with tassels and plumes in one place or another. Napoleon's imperial guard flourished gold tassels. The French Foreign Legion's red epaulets and tassels signify a "baptism of fire." Soldiers in the Greek army's Evzones regiment, who serve as the royal guard at the palace in Athens, wear white, pleated wool skirts, pompons on their shoes, and a tasseled red fez, as they have for centuries.

The kilt, probably brought to Scotland by a Greek soldier over two thousand years ago, was originally used as a blanket at night and then pleated about the body during the day. To compensate for the kilt's lack of pockets, the sporran pouch—with its decorative tassels—was created. In wartime, officers wore a red cloth sash over their left shoulder with tassels on the end; when they were wounded, the sash was used to pull them off the battlefield. The common soldier had no such advantage. Today the tasseled red sash is worn only by the Pipe Major in a Scottish band. Pipers' uniforms include shoelaces that are tied around the ankle and leg; these have rolled-leather tassels on their tips.

The fez and tassel were adopted in 1827 as the official non-Christian headdress in Turkey. Even after the collapse of the sultanate in 1919, the Turkish soldier of the mighty Ottoman Empire retained his red felt fez with its gold tassel and his peak-toed shoes with their gold pompons. His girlfriend might wear a gold embroidered fez with a long blue tassel.

Spanish bullfighter's jacket

Shriners (and tassels) on parade

Any book on military dress will attest that tassels have served their nations well in wartime. In times of peace, military honor guards throughout the world stand ready with tassels by their sides.

Although not a military organization, the Ancient Arabic Order of Nobles of the Mystic Shrine, otherwise known as the Shriners, adopted the fez and tassel as their official hat. The real power of the Shriners' black tassel lies in the remarkable job those who wear it have done in providing care through their hospitals for over 400,000 crippled and burned children.

Warriors of a different nature are often fortified with tassels to do battle against their respective foes. In Japan, sumo wrestlers frequently sport large tassels on their traditional mawashi aprons as they stomp about the ring. Fire fighters in that country placed large, white cloth tassels on a long pole at the center of a fire. Each brigade displayed its own standard and directed the action from the pole.

At bullfights it is a banderillero's job to place a pair of tasseled darts in the bull's neck or shoulder muscles before the matador appears to face his adversary. The matador's short silk or velvet jacket is grandly trimmed with gold braid, jewels, embroidery, and tassels, and his tight-fitting pants are secured just below the knee by tassels called "machos" (an apt name for a power tassel).

Kings and queens have long applied the tassel to their symbols of authority. A faience collar excavated from the tomb of Tutankhamen (king of Egypt from 1366 to 1357 B.C.) shows tassels on the ends of the cords used as closures.

The Assyrians were probably the first to use tassels as badges of honor, but the practice has continued and today tassels adorn royal flags and other insignias of state. The imperial robe worn by Queen Elizabeth II at her coronation in 1953 was resplendent with large gold tassels; her palace guards stood tall in black-tasseled helmets. The wardens of the Tower of London and the yeomen of the guard still wear the medieval uniform and carry the gold-tasseled lance, while the Lord Chancellor of England carries the seal of state in a tasseled bag. A long, plumed tassel tops the helmet of the royal horse guard. The Jordanian royal family raises purebred Arabian horses and decorates them with cascades of tassels.

Left: Silk and metal tassels embellish this eighteenth century purse used to carry the Great Seal of England.

Top right: British yeomen of the guard at the Tower of London

Bottom right: Queen of England's royal guards

Since 1970 Dr. Hastings Kamuzu Banda—Life President of the African Republic of Malawi—has performed his official functions in Western dress but has carried a tassel fly-whisk, long a symbol of African authority. Some whisks are simply horse or cow hair woven or braided onto a stick, while on others the tail of the animal is docked, and its bone becomes a part of the tassel.

During a river parade to celebrate his birthday, the king of Thailand enjoys a ceremonial barge which is carved from a single tree forty-six meters long and which weighs almost thirteen tons; it requires a crew of sixty-four oarsmen. In its midsection rests a throne for the king and queen, and on its bow is carved the shape of a mythical bird with a large, heavily ornamented tassel hanging from its mouth. Other boats in the parade have tassels, but the king's is always the grandest.

Paintings of the Chinese philosopher Confucius show him wearing tassels. In Korea the king presented bags of roasted beans wrapped in red paper and hung with tassels—which served to repel evil spirits—to his relatives during the first lunar month. On the fifth day of the fifth month, he gave his subjects fans with medicine tied onto a tasseled pendant, thus insuring a healthy populace.

No one quite knows how man first reached the Americas, but the arid wastes of northern Mexico separated all but the most nomadic people from what is now the United States. The Indians of Central America developed a 365-day solar calendar and a system of hieroglyphic writing. They wrote and drew on pieces of deerskin or maquey-bark paper—seven inches wide by sixteen feet in length—which were then folded into books that opened like a screen. Most of these early sacred codices were destroyed by the Spanish, but those that survive provide important information about the lives and customs of pre-Columbian times.

These codices and the carved, stylized, maize plant designs on ruins and tombs indicate that the basis of the early Indian diet was corn, a plant which played an important role in the history and development of pre-Hispanic meso-America. What all this has to do with tassels is that in order for kernels to develop on its cob, each individual silk thread of the corn plant must be fertilized by the pollen-bearing tassel.

Opposite page: King of Thailand's ceremonial barge

Above: Carving dated 667 B.C. shows tassels worn by ancient Mayans. (Piedras Negras, Guatemala)

umes are used today in festival dances, but the lordly plumes are replaced with yarn pompons and the tasseled loincloth with blue jeans. The massive headdress worn in the plume dance of Oaxaca is heavily embellished with pompons and tassels.

Replicas of ceramic figures found in tombs—often sold as "genuine antiques"—and costumed doll curios made for the tourist trade offer additional evidence that tassels were a part of ancient raiment.

Around 1500 B.C., artistic techniques appeared, and by 100 B.C., glyph writing was in use in the Mayan, Zapotec, and Nahau ceremonial centers. Stone carvings, wood lintels, decorated ceramic figures, and bowls from early tombs reveal the extent to which culture had developed. A carved lintel, circa A.D. 700, depicts the presentation of an offering to an elaborately dressed priest. Both the offering—which is similar to Native American medicine bundles—and the priest are decorated with tassels. A lintel arch from Piedras Negras in Central America, dated 667 B.C., has many figures with tasseled aprons and beaded, tasseled neckpieces. Another at Ceibal Peten, dated 810 B.C., clearly displays a loincloth weighted by a large tassel. Carvings of the Mayan water goddess Ixchel depict tassels on her garments, an appropriate touch since she is also the goddess of weaving and childbirth.

At Bonampak in Chiapas, a Mayan mural painting includes tassels along with the sacred jaguar figure. The

Finding the exact origin of the corn plant has occupied botanists and archaeologists for years. Fossil pollen grains discovered in a valley in Mexico reveal that the corn tassel has been around for at least eighty thousand years. Now that's a power tassel!

Domestication and man's use of corn is thought to have occurred in the Oaxaca area of Mexico between 5000 and 1000 B.C. Corn cultivation made it unnecessary for tribes to move from place to place in search of food. With the advent of agriculture, villages evolved. Once settled in permanent homes, the people of early civilizations developed ceramics and weaving; their burial sites preserve evidence of these activities. Eventually cities were formed. All because of the corn tassel!

Stylized drawings on codices show forms that look like tassels appearing in likely places: on tunics, footwear, cinctures, headdresses, and garters. When they performed rituals, high priests and deities were outfitted with elaborate feathered capes and headdresses. Similar cos-

This tasseled figure stands guard in front of the Archaeology Museum in Guatemala City.

Mayans believed that their priests, or "h'men," received enlightenment from the gods which enabled them to make cosmic forces work for the good of mankind. These priests' loincloths are embellished with rows of tassels. According to the codices, plumed or tasseled serpents are life-giving performers of miracles.

The Aztecs believed that corn originated as a gift from the god Quetzalcoatl, who first created man from his own blood and then turned himself into an ant to obtain a kernel of corn hidden inside a mountain. Without this grain from the god, man would have been unable to start the first civilization. In one Aztec carving, Tezcatlipoca—the god who brought about the demise of Quetzalcoatl—is shown wearing a vest tied with tasseled cords. Legend says that Quetzalcoatl now lives in the heavens in the form of the planet Venus.

Aztec gods demanded special ceremonies and sacrifices, which included tearing out the beating heart of the bravest prisoner of war. Distinctive stones were carved

Draped Christ figure (Mexico)

Christ figure (Mexico)

for this purpose. One—the sacrificial stone of Tizoc, the ruler of the Aztecs in 1481—shows his victorious tasseled warriors leading captives by the hair. This stone is eight feet in diameter with a depression in the center to receive the heart. No one knows what part the tassel played in this ritual, but I don't think I would have gone without mine on ceremonial days!

Cortez invaded Mexico in 1519 and eventually conquered the Aztecs. Soon, indigenous rituals were replaced by the religious statues and trappings of Catholicism. Churches were built on the ruins of ancient cultures. Nuns and priests were sent to convert the Indians. The churches were covered with gold, and the statues were dressed in royal clothing complete with gold tassels and cords.

Today in wayside shrines, tiny chapels, and magnificent cathedrals all over Mexico, images of Christ, the Virgin Mary, and lesser saints are venerated and adored. Each is displayed in a suitable costume resplendent with tassels. The more important figures may have a wardrobe of a dozen or more costumes, which are changed periodically depending on the occasion.

Religious articles representing a mix of Indian and Catholic beliefs are sold outside many Mexican churches.

An amulet protects, a talisman brings good fortune, and ex-votos are given in thanks for blessings received. Regardless of their purpose, many have a tassel or pompon attached.

The Ojos de Venado (eye of the deer) is an amulet made from a seed pod; a holy picture and a red pompon are glued on it. Sometimes a few beads are added, making a bracelet for small children to wear as protection against those who might look into their eyes and lead them astray. Light-eyed, pretty females are thought to be particularly susceptible. Fear of the "evil eye" occurs in many cultures, and tassels seem to offer protection.

From birth to death in almost all societies, tassels are thought to add power or renown to our lives. As a final gesture of recognition, tassels are often carved on tomb-stones and are commonly found on hearses and biers from Singapore to San Francisco.

Top: Mexican amulet tassels represent a mix of Indian and Catholic beliefs.

Bottom: Carved tassels on a tombstone (California)

Tassels: The Fanciful Embellishment

Personal Tassels

T assels are truly a celebration of the superfluous. While those used by shamans and priests impart power, others compose a silent and personal statement for their owners. Notice the tassels dangling from the rearview mirrors of cars and buses the world over. Each of these holds a special place in the driver's eyes. Mere ornament? Maybe not. The graduation tassel in a car is certainly a symbol of personal achievement to its owner; in a bus, the tasseled plastic charm hanging from the mirror must have some significance to the driver. The Christian cross with a Chinese tassel and Korean knot that I spied in an Indonesian taxi expressed at least a cross-cultural outlook. A taxi driver in Turkey assures his own safety and that of his passengers with a miniature Koran enclosed in a purple tassel. All these swaying tassels surely have a personal meaning for the person who put them there. That often seems to be the way with tassels.

Left: After cleansing and purifying themselves, Indian women line up to enter a temple. Decorative tassels are braided into their hair.

Above: Personal rearview mirror tassel

In 1977 I assigned tassels as a beginning project in my fiber arts classes as a simple way to explore color, texture, and form. What a thrill I had in store! Those wonderfully creative students produced miniature works of art—far from simple—showing a depth and feeling seldom seen in an assignment. I wish I had recorded them all because through the years I've forgotten many, but I thank each of those students for introducing me to the personal world of tassels.

One student—a lovely Italian grandmother who spoke almost no English—took from my bag of supplies a

A mother's memento, created from her children's hair

jumbled heap of yellow rayon threads that should have been tossed out. It must have taken her hours to untangle the mess and then crochet a lei of tassels. No language barrier existed in the warm and tender hug she gave me when she turned in her assignment as a gift.

A busy, almost frantic mother of four active children, who was taking the class during her only free time, always had to leave early to meet the school bus. She didn't have time to shop for yarn, but as she was cutting her children's hair, she noticed the various colors collecting on the floor. She braided all the hair together and wrapped it with red thread to form a very personal tassel. I spoke to her recently and learned that one of her children had died; I hope she still has the tassel.

A young freshman who had little money and less interest in school signed up looking for an easy class. Whether she made a special trip to her favorite thrift store or used part of her own rummaged wardrobe, I will never know, but the tassel she submitted was spectacular. She had unravelled an old white sweater and created from it a wonderful, crinkly, curly, fuzzy tassel. She got a huge hand from the class (and maybe decided that school wasn't so bad after all).

An older class member, who also frequented thrift shops, had a splendid knack for combining seemingly incompatible items; her sense of color and style enabled her to effectively combine "bargains" that most of us would have overlooked. Recently widowed, she had decided to treat herself to a new outfit, but no somber black or grey would do. This clever woman managed to unify a fuchsia print skirt (too large for her) and a shocking-pink sweater (which didn't match at all), by combining excess fabric from the skirt and yarn from the sweater ribbing into a very long, wide tasseled belt. The effect was sensational.

And so it went. On that autumn afternoon, twenty-five men and women each took a simple assignment and created a very personal statement.

When I asked clothing designer Anita Mayer how she viewed tassels, she shared this personal story: "As I worked on my garment...as my hands made tassels and my fingers wrapped and tied, I thought about Nonna, my Yugoslavian grandmother. Although she never learned to speak English, and I never spoke Yugoslavian, there was a connection between us that transcended language and age. My fascination with clothing from the Slavic states began with the books Nonna shared with me... photographs and drawings of elegant men and women

Anita Mayer's **Homage to my Yugoslavian Grandmother**

proudly wearing magnificent garments made with love and care. Although I learned to weave long after her death, I knew that one day I would honor Nonna with a piece created out of our shared heritage. *Homage to my Yugoslavian Grandmother* is my gift to her....The tassels connect generations and cultures."

I was equally touched when a woman sent me a photograph of the last piece of art her mother had made for her. Her mother, she wrote, had been an artist all her life and in spite of illness had managed to make her a wonderful "light and sound" tassel just before she died. The tassel's skirt was threaded with bits of metal and mirror that reflected light onto the walls as the tassel moved. Antique copper Indian bells provided sound as they bumped melodically against Mexican milagros. (Milagros, the Spanish word for miracles, are metal charms shaped like parts of the body. The charms are placed in churches as prayers for healing.) The twinkle and tone from this tassel created its own small miracle—a message of love from mother to daughter.

The personal tassel is one that represents or celebrates something important to the individual. And what is worth celebrating more than love? As Cupid's companion, tassels play a romantic role. They are often attached to love tokens such as valentines. The idea dates back to A.D. 269, when a Roman emperor decided that bachelors made better soldiers and forbade men to marry. A Christian priest named Valentine defied the law by continuing to perform marriages until he was executed, thus becoming the patron saint of lovers.

Today tassels accompany many to the altar. In central Asia, a Turkoman bride's face is completely covered by a high crowned headdress adorned with wrapped and beaded tassels; her counterpart in a Japanese Shinto ceremony leaves her face visible, but her red-lined bridal kimono, fan, and elaborate bridal hat are all tasseled. The hours-long Hindu wedding pageant entails a sacred fire and long tasseled crowns worn by both bride and groom. In Mexico, couples may be bound together with a tasseled satin rope as they kneel at the altar.

The Druse, an Arabic-speaking tribe living in Syria and Lebanon, practice a secret religion. During her childhood, a girl weaves and embroiders a wedding dress which is presented to the bridegroom, whom she has never met, one hour before the wedding. All the leftover embroidery threads are gathered into tassels to decorate the arm and neck closures.

A collection of tassel-trimmed, miniature hats from the Middle East has a long and romantic history. These hats were made around 1875 by children at a Palestinian orphanage. In 1918 William Yale, a descendant of the founder of Yale University, bought them as a gift for his

Miniature hats made in a Palestinian orphanage (1875)

beloved as a reminder of the "happy day in Jerusalem when we met."

In India a married woman is likely to wear a tasseled nose ring (the directions for which will not be covered here). Moroccan women perform a ritual love dance for their men with a tasseled and beaded necklace. (No directions for this one either!) A Mien bride from northern Laos wears a huge structure over her head for two days and two nights of the eight-day wedding ceremony. Over this heavy framework are placed heirloom embroidered cloths with tassels on the corners; a lengthy strip covered with many long red tassels with black and white beads is tied over the whole structure.

The clothing we wear is a personal matter, defined in part by the particular culture to which we belong. Tassels are seldom a lone individual's choice. They are either "in style" or not worn. Southeast Asia is one area where tassels are very much the style.

Top: Mien baby's cap

Bottom: This tasseled piece will embellish the elaborate head-dress worn by a Mien woman at her wedding.

Mien or Yao women of Laos are known for their exquisite embroidery and tassels. A dark ankle-length coat with red pompon ruff is worn with embroidered pants. The coat is slit to the waist, and red silk or wool tassels fill in the slit. On special occasions, a below-waist-length, red silk tassel with silver top hangs down the back of the coat; various silver pendants, beads, bells, and balls dangle from it.

Mien babies, starting at age one, wear delightful little caps embellished with embroidery, appliqué, pompons, and tassels. Girls wear caps with a large donut-shaped pompon on top. Tassels and other items may be suspended from the center of the pompon. Boys have round pompons on the top and sides of an appliquéd cap. Men's jackets are also decorated with embroidery, fingerbraids, and tassels.

The Lisu hill people of Thailand loop spectacular tassels over their sashes. The clusters of long, multicolored strips of fabric have small wool pompons at the ends. Each set may have as many as five hundred strands and pompons. At Chinese New Year dances, where young men and women have a chance to meet one another, both sexes wear these. Red-tasseled silver earrings and masses of colorful yarn with beads and pompons are added to the attire. It seems as if the more silver and tassels one can pile on, the more desirable one will be.

Guatemala is another country famous for beautiful textiles. The color and vibrancy of its intricate weaving and exquisite embroidery is punctuated by brilliant tassels and pompons. Twenty languages and over two hundred ethnic groups exist in the Mayan culture; traditional dress serves to identify an Indian with his group. Each community has distinctive clothing which may reveal the age, sex, and social rank of the wearer as well as announce the occasion for which each costume is worn.

Mayan women weave on backstrap or stick looms, just as their ancestors did, but commercial thread has now replaced hand-dyed and spun yarn. Tassels and pompons, even if acrylic, are still a part of most traditional dress. They are wrapped into the hair, dangled from ears, draped around the waist, attached to shawls and scarves, and are worn by men, women, and children. They decorate statues and crosses in church. Cars and trucks are

Left: Lisu hill tribe New Year's tassel (Thailand)

Below: Tasseled Akha women (Thailand)

bedecked with tassels too. I'll never forget one truck I saw with the message "God is Love" spelled out in pompons across the windshield. Tassels hung from the rearview mirror, and pompon fringe decorated the other windows.

In Korea it was customary for a bride to present embroidered "bags of filial duty" to her in-laws. The closures were elaborately knotted and tasseled to demonstrate her skill at this traditional craft. There are never four tassels on these, however, since that number is considered to be just as unlucky as some people believe the number thirteen to be.

Tassels born of love exist the world over. Two California women's love for their first grandchildren—and for tassels, of course—resulted in a tasseled baby quilt,

This page and opposite page: Guatemalan women

designed to be used as a canopy for the first few months of life. The tassels furnish bright and stimulating color for young eyes. When the child is older, the quilt converts to a cuddle-up blanket; stroking its tassels brings the sandman quickly!

Barbara Leet, a more experienced grandmother, keeps in her office a board covered with marvellous tassels that she has made, purchased, or received. "My little grand-daughter," she says, "has spent more time playing with tassels than with anything she has here—sometimes they become people, are sorted by size, and are given names. She may even dress them in Barbie doll clothes. Sometimes they decorate the shrubs in the yard, and sometimes they adorn her; small gold tassels make perfect earrings for an Egyptian costume. When she was a toddler, we used a big fluffy one to keep a balloon string at floor level. All grandmothers should have tassels. Besides, they make great package ties or napkin rings.

And using up all the color-coordinated yarns from stitching projects to make tassels keeps the yarns from cluttering up my shelves."

Do you have a collection of stuff you can't use but can't bring yourself to throw away? I used to, until I realized that all this flotsam and jetsam of my life would fit nicely into a tassel. Now I pin or tie these extraneous items to my "life tassel," which hangs in the laundry room. No one else sees it, but it reminds me of the many happy pieces of my life.

My "life tassel" started out as a lampshade that somehow got burned, stained, and then torn until there wasn't a side left to turn to the wall. It ended up in the garage along with other things that I couldn't throw out (or someone else had). A few years (and garages) later, I uncovered both the wire frame and some purple and turquoise cording. I hung the colorful strands from the frame and formed a tassel for the odds and ends I treasure. On it are hand-stitched name tags from meetings, souvenir pins and badges from places I have visited, dog tags, house and car keys from long ago, a leftover earring, a broken bracelet, tiny notes, and loving postcards from friends—all things I'm now glad I didn't discard.

You don't need a bride, groom, grandchild, or a cluttered garage in your life to make and enjoy personal tassels. You might start with one of the following:

A travel tassel: Do you collect small objects while you're on the road—things that seem important at the time but which just get in the way once you get them home? Such souvenirs make great reminders of your trips and are perfect components for a tassel. I have a friend who finds buttons on the street and in shops when she travels and incorporates them into a tassel.

A celebration tassel: Whether your child has just left for kindergarten or college, you're likely to be left with that inevitable pile of remaining trash (or treasure, depending on your point of view). You can either throw it out or make a celebration tassel for yourself or your child. (One of you will surely be celebrating.)

An identification tassel: Give them to your traveling friends to put on their luggage. Then, when the suitcases come around on the airport carousel, your tassel will be easy to spot. Some tour companies provide their participants with matching bags or backpacks. A bright tassel will help you spot yours in the inevitable hotel-lobby pile. When traveling with a small group, give each person a different colored tassel to ensure that you each end up with your own toothbrush. Nylon and plastic tassels are

Above: Alix Peshette trims her horse with tassels.

Top left and right: Bride's tassels

Above: Dictionary tassel

great on white water rafting bags. Just as Peruvian llama owners identify their animals by placing tassels in their ears, Alix Peshette of Sacramento, California, uses tassels to distinguish her horse.

An award tassel: A tassel can be presented as an award or prize and is much more interesting than a standard "blue ribbon." Pin a tassel to the winner's work at your next show, or better yet, give one to each participant. Surprise a child with a tassel for a clean room or as a certificate for some achievement. Can't you think of a lot of people who deserve a special award? While you're at it, make one for yourself.

A wedding tassel: Make your bridal gift a little more special by including a tassel. Create a tassel out of "something old, something new, something borrowed, and something blue" to tuck in the bride's bouquet, or make a white satin, lace, and pearl tassel for her wed-

ding banner. Remember the mothers and grandmothers with a pretty tassel that will match their dresses and complement their corsages. A tassel will last long after the flowers have wilted and will be a reminder of the happy occasion.

A gift tassel: For birthdays, holidays, and anniversaries of all kinds, a resplendent tassel is a touch of thoughtfulness that won't violate the "no presents, please" request. At Christmas, why not exchange a tassel instead of an ornament or gift? Or simply write a message on a piece of fancy paper, add some yarn, roll it up, and fringe the ends. Tie a bow at the neck and you have a tassel greet-

ing. A similar idea was used in eighteenth century European "distaff letters." Young men decorated long narrow strips of parchment with painted flowers, hearts, and poems; these romantic notes were rolled tightly, tied with ribbon, and slipped into the flax on the distaff of a young lady's spinning wheel. Think what an extraordinary tassel book you could write this way. (Of course, tassels themselves make great bookmarks.)

For a particularly dreaded birthday, Jean Goldberg fashioned a rock-and-roll tassel to twirl to blaring music. Jean's is made with cassette tape and incorporates her birthstone, the Australian amethyst. Whether you're turning thirty or ninety, you're never too old to take up tassel twirling!

When Margery Williams retired as a local chapter president of the Embroiderers Guild of America, each member made her a tassel for her sewing basket. One tassel had tiny baskets attached, each with its own minuscule tassel. Pennye Kurtela not only trims baskets, but personalizes "belts, jewelry, jackets, dresses, coats, bags, and all the walls in every room of my house with tassels." Candace Kling created a very personal, contemporary headdress incorporating vintage tassels from the sash of a turn-of-the-century gown.

Tassels really are a perfect gift or project. Whether the ones you make represent quick statements or life stories, each will add a personal touch to the world of tassels.

Above: Candace Kling's contemporary "Red Rainbow" headdress incorporates vintage tassels.

Right: Penny Kurtela's tasseled basket

The Key to Tassels

As tassel makers have for centuries, we can all create romance, magic, or miracles. Tassels are tactile objects, fun to hold and to handle, and the best way to enjoy them is to make your own. Inspiration can come from the heart or the thrift store. As you begin to create your tassels, let your imagination off its leash—forget preconceived notions. There is no rule that says you "should" (you "should" use yarn), and there is no rule that says you "can't" (you "can't" make a tassel).

If you're stuck for an idea, stand on your head or climb a tree—ALTER YOUR PERSPECTIVE!

If no design comes to mind, take a walk until you find four things that intrigue you; remember, ideas are things too—SEE WITH NEW EYES!

Whatever you do—unless it keeps the sun from rising—it isn't a disaster. What you think is a mistake might really be a creative opportunity. Dan Stanford says, "Experience is what you get when you don't get what you want." I've read somewhere that if you try to do something and fail, you are much better off than if you try to do nothing and succeed. Will Rogers put it this way: "Even if you're on the right track, you'll get run over if you just sit there." So let's get to tasseling!

The key to constructing successful tassels lies in understanding a few simple techniques. Thread your way through the "key holders" in this chapter; the methods described in them can be combined in a multitude of ways to create all types of tassels. Once you master the basics, the possibilities are endless.

If you've ever spent an exasperating few minutes fishing for keys in the bottom of your purse, or if you've

Key tassel for a bookcase

Top left and right: Special-key tassels

Bottom: Car key tassel

"lost" a special key in a drawer full of debris, you'll welcome the tassel. It's easy to keep track of car keys once a bright, sassy tassel is attached to them. A silky-soft, elegantly tasseled key will add grace and charm as it hangs on a handsome cupboard or box. And what about a front-door key tassel to match the color of your house? Or a back-door key tassel in a wonderful combination of colors that you've never tried before?

Key tassels were originally used by the privileged classes of Europe to identify the various keys with which they locked cupboards against pilfering servants. Master furniture carver James McGarry of Australia says, "All of my furniture keys wear tassels. They'd look naked without them. A key without a tassel is like a meal without wine or a day without love."

If you're lacking keys (or servants who pilfer), you can fill a basket with colorful tassels and pompons for pure visual and sensual delight. Tassels can be enjoyed in hundreds of ways whether you use them or not. Just making them is a pleasure.

This chapter describes general construction techniques. Instructions are not intended to produce the same tassel for everyone, so each tassel you make will be uniquely your own. You will decide how big or how long to make it and what colors and textures to use. The projects are merely starting points; they offer simple ideas for you to put together in your own creative way. With them, you can give your home and yourself a lift—to the limits of your imagination and ingenuity.

Creating Tassels

SPECIAL-KEY TASSEL

We'll start by making a tassel to identify a "special key" for a china cabinet or armoire. As you select the yarns, keep in mind the decor of the room where the tasseled key will go. Of course, if you can't find a key, think about updating your window shades, lamp and drawer pulls, or a ceiling fan with a tassel or two.

Selecting Materials

Materials should be chosen to suit their use. For a key ring that you'll carry every day, sturdy yarns are essential. For a special-key holder that is mainly decorative, more luxurious fibers can be used. Each fiber has its own personality.

Wool is wonderful and behaves well in most situations. It can be washed and felted, unplied for a fluffier look, or tightly bound to "poof out." Beware of overspun rug wool, however; although it wears exceedingly well, it lacks the bounce and spring that make a nice tassel.

Rayon and silk make great slinky, shiny, sleek tassels, but the tassel and fiber will quickly work themselves into a mess if they aren't handled carefully. Both these fibers take dye exceedingly well, producing a range of lustrous colors.

Linen is stiff and tends to stick together. Excessive handling makes it fuzzy, but it is strong and weathers well outdoors. Linen lasts; in fact, linens over seven thousand years old have been unearthed during archaeological expeditions. If you're making a tassel for your casket, this is the material to choose!

Many metallic threads will stand out stiffly, so choose a soft variety for winding (unless you want a tassel that can't decide which end is up).

Man-made fibers and blends all have their place, and no rule exists that says you can't mix materials in a tassel. You aren't likely to throw it in the washing machine or dryer.

The use, the drape, and the color are your main considerations when selecting fibers for a tassel. Think about where your tassel will be seen and the conditions it's likely to encounter. Hold different weights and textures to see how they hang. Then try various color combinations until you're satisfied with the results.

You aren't limited to yarn. The effect you have in mind may call for strips of cloth, ribbons, or strands of beads. Hair, fur, raffia, or strips of leather give a primitive look.

Top: Leather tassels embellish a vest

Bottom: Rolled leather tassels (Africa)

Experiment. The idea of a "string too short to save" doesn't apply to tassels. Even the tiniest scrap of yarn or ribbon can make a mighty statement when set off in a tassel.

Twisting a Hanging Cord

Whatever materials you choose, a handsome tassel deserves a sturdy cord from which to hang.

- Select one or more of the stronger yarns you have chosen for your special-key tassel.

- Measure this yarn about six times longer than the length of the desired cord. Shrinkage in the finished length will be determined by the type of yarn used and by how tightly it is twisted. If the cord is too long you can cut it off, but you can't make it longer.

- Fold the yarns in half, and tie the cut ends together so you have a loop.

- Hold the loop between the index fingers of each hand and start twisting. If you are particularly dexterous, one finger can twist in one direction and the other finger in the opposite. (Just be sure one finger doesn't untwist.) Until you master this motion, let one finger do the twisting until the yarns begin to kink. Release the tension slightly to check. The yarns should twist back on themselves. It's better to overtwist a bit.

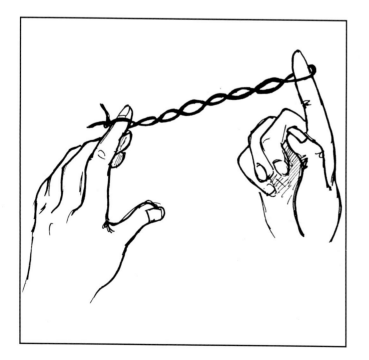

- Slip the special key to the center of the twisted yarns (your teeth or a friend would be handy at this point).

- Fold the yarns in half with the key caught in the center and twist in the opposite direction to form a smooth cord. (Of course you can simply make the cord by itself and loop the key through it later.)

- Tie a secure knot in the cut end to prevent the cord from unwinding. Any knot will do. An overhand one is neat and easy and will not show since it will be covered by the wrapping on the tassel. The cord can be shortened by tying the knot higher; the excess length can be trimmed or left to form part of the tassel skirt.

Lay the cord and key aside and read through the rest of this section. Jot down the ideas that appeal to you and choose the way you would like to wind your tassel. Attach the cord, wrap the neck, and trim the ends. Take pleasure in your own special-key tassel.

Winding a Tassel

Select any firm surface to use as a form—cardboard, this book, your elbow, or your fingers—and wind the chosen yarn (or yarns) around it. The form for a tassel should be about 1/2" (1.25 cm) longer than its finished length. If in doubt, make it a little longer and trim it to size. No magic formula exists for the number of times to wrap the yarn; your taste is the determining factor. The yarns do not have to line up with each other, so wrap freely. The more yarn, the fuller the tassel.

Attaching the Cord

- Cut the ends of the tassel yarns along one edge of the form and lay the yarns out flat.

- Place the cord in the middle of (and parallel to) the yarns with the knot well below the center.

- Work the yarns evenly around the knotted end of the cord. Tie securely with strong yarn above the knot.

- Bring the upper yarns down over the lower ones and wrap above the knot to form a neck. Keeping the knot below the wrapping helps to anchor it.

Options:

- Put the tassel yarns through the looped, knotted end of the cord. Wrap and trim. Or if you have an attractive knot, make it a focal point by placing it at the top of the tassel; use the ends below the knot to tie the cord to the tassel (inside the head).

- Anchor tassels securely to the holding cord; they must be able to withstand the fondling or tugging they're sure to receive.

- If you choose not to use a hanger, the tassel yarns can be folded over a dowel or pencil until wrapped. Or for a tidy finish, slip a small cord through the top of the wound yarn. Slide the knotted end of the cord through the looped end and pull tightly. Place the knotted end of the cord inside the tassel yarns and wrap the neck.

Wrapping the Neck

Wrapping is necessary to secure the yarns but is also a great way to personalize a tassel. Wrapping provides a way to add color, a means of shaping, and an area for embellishing. There are no set rules; if you don't like the effect, you can unwrap in a jiffy.

- Arrange the tassel yarns you wound to form a neat and symmetrical head.

- Select wrapping yarn and hold one end well below the area to be wrapped. If the color blends with the skirt, this end will become a part of the tassel. Otherwise, cut it off after it is wrapped.

- Decide where the top of the tassel neck is to be and wrap once tightly around all of the tassel yarns. Check to see that all the yarns in the head and skirt are exactly where you want them and then proceed with the wrapping. The secret here is to lay each round neatly and tightly next to the other.

Following are several ways to make a smooth and neat wrapping with the ends securely fastened and out of sight:

Tapestry Needle

- Hold one end of the wrapping yarn over the area of the tassel to be wrapped.

- With the other end, wrap over it a few turns to secure.

- Lay in a tapestry needle with the eye pointing down.

- Wrap tightly over the needle to complete the neck.

- Thread wrapping yarn into the eye and pull the needle and yarn all the way through the wrapped area.

- Clip off the end so it's even with the wrapped area.

Yarn Needle

- You can make a "needle" by forming a loop out of any strong, smooth string or yarn and laying it below the area to be wrapped. Leave the ends of the string sticking above the wrapping.

- Wrap over the yarn needle as far as you want, then put the end of the wrapping yarn through the loop and pull up on both ends of the yarn needle to remove it completely.

- Clip the end of the wrapping yarn.

(A permanent, sturdy "needle eye" can be made with a short loop of fishing line threaded through a button. The button makes it easy to pull.)

Peruvian Method

The wrapping yarn itself can form a needle, like those used in Peru, but the yarn must be smooth and strong for this method to work.

- Hold the yarn parallel to and against the tassel with an inch or so extending above the area to be wrapped and the rest hanging below it. Use this longer end to form a loop that extends below the area to be wrapped. Then bring it back up and take a turn around the upper part of the tassel so that this first wrap locks the loop in place.

- Continue wrapping down the tassel to the desired neck length.

- When you get to the bottom, insert the end of the yarn into the loop and gently pull on the top end just enough to secure the loop and yarn inside the wrapped area. (Don't pull all the way through.) One end will extend above the wrapping and one below. Clip them both off.

Advanced Planning Methods

- Dental floss threaders from the drugstore have a loop of strong nylon that forms a handy needle. One brand is "Butler EEZ-Thru."

- Some commercial tassels are held together by a wrapped metal "staple." To make your own, cover a wide metal band with yarn, fold it over the tassel yarns, tuck in the ends, and whack it into place. Graduation tassels are held in place with a wide metal cylinder to which a charm of the appropriate year is added.

Winding Multiple Tassels

Many special-key tassels are made using lots of little tassels strung together.

- Use a wider form and wind as many tassels at one time as you will need. Count the number of wraps in order to make each tassel the same size.

- String a cord or ribbon through the top of each bundle (Fig. 1). Carefully cut off one tassel and wrap the neck to secure it to the cord.

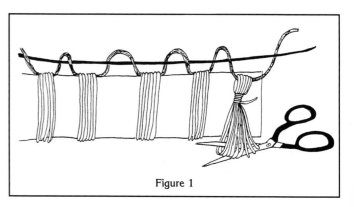

Figure 1

- Then cut off the next tassel and wrap again before proceeding to the next one.

- When all the tassels are wrapped, gather up the cord's loops on thin wire or strong thread and attach them to a mold or to the neck of a larger tassel. Wrap over the wire to keep it from showing. You can make two or three rows of these little tassels (Fig. 2).

Figure 2

This method of winding is also useful for making tassels for the four corners of a pillow (Fig. 3). Instead of stringing them on a cord, tie each bundle of tassel yarns on one end with

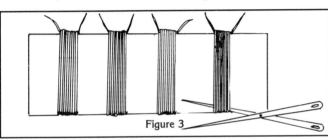

Figure 3

Figure 4

a strong heavy yarn, then cut the other ends of yarn (or don't cut and just bend the cardboard form to remove, leaving the loops). Continue to tie knots one on top of the other to create a strong holding cord. The knots will make the tassel hang nicely, too. The ends of the tying yarn can then be used to sew the tassel directly to the pillow (Fig. 4).

Winding Circular Tassels

- Wrap yarn continuously on a long piece of soft cardboard over a thin wire or a piece of matching yarn.

- Slip out the cardboard and gather the wire to fit around the hanging cord or a form.

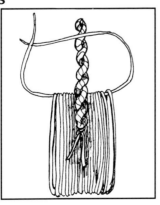

- Wrap the neck securely. This forms a circular tassel with a closed fringe.

Winding Striped Tassels

For a striped tassel, wind separate colors—a section of one color with a section of another color next to it. Each section will make two stripes. Here are some ideas for striped tassels:

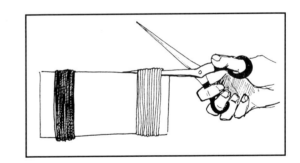

All-American Tassel

- Start by winding a white group of yarns.

- Then wind a red group next to it and cut the bottoms.

- Cross the red group over the white group and attach to a twisted cord or tie off as for pillow tassels.

- Wrap a wide neck with blue yarn, add some gold French knots, and you have the all-American tassel!

Rainbow Tassel

- Wind all the colors of the rainbow, one on top of the other, and wrap the neck.

- Cut away each stripe in staggered layers on one side of the tassel only. The same effect can be achieved by cutting the colors in varying lengths and layering them over one another before wrapping.

That wraps up this section except for a few loose ends. I hope you've found ideas to make a fitting tassel for your special key.

Loose Ends

- You can trim the bottom of the tassel so it's rounded for a jaunty look or trim it at an angle for a sleek, sophisticated look.

- Three-ply yarns, such as Persian wool, can be unplied to make a fuller, fluffier skirt after wrapping.

- The head of a tassel can be made fuller and rounder by inserting a bead or marble and wrapping the neck securely around it. Stuffing can be used, but be sure it matches the yarn because bits and pieces may protrude.

- If you pull down sharply on the inner core of yarns in the tassel while holding the neck, the outer yarns in the head will puff out.

CAR KEY TASSEL

When you're ready to try another tassel, you can accommodate a cluster of keys by working a tassel over a purchased key ring. Since this tassel will be handled a lot, choose tightly plied yarns that won't fuzz or fray. Try unusual color combinations, or if you've had your colors analyzed, use your palette and the key ring will provide an easy reference. The colors can be mixed by winding them all together, or each color can be wound separately to form stripes.

Choose enough yarn to make about a 1-1/2" (3.75 cm) clump approximately 20" (50 cm) long. You've probably figured out by now that there are no exact guidelines; you'll have a much more interesting tassel if you go with your instincts.

Tassel on a Holder

Anything that has a hole in it will accommodate a tassel. For our purposes, use a separating ring from a hardware or variety store. Your keys can be put directly on this ring, or another key ring can be inserted onto the tassel ring.

- Pull a selection of yarns through the ring so that about 1/3 of the length is on one side (Fig. 1). This will be approximately the finished length of the tassel. The longer yarns on the other side will be the working ones.

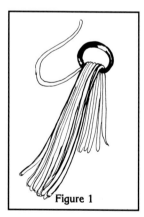

Figure 1

- Pick up one of the long yarns and use it to wrap tightly just below the ring. This secures all the strands to the ring.

- Wrap as you wish, picking up a working yarn, wrapping awhile, and then dropping it back into the body of the tassel. Any color can be used and then exchanged with any of the other working yarns by wrapping and returning it to the body of the tassel as you complete each color.

- When you finish the entire wrapped section, secure the end (Fig. 2).

Yarn Beads

- Try adding a yarn bead to your tassel by taking a few of the working yarns and wrapping them horizontally around all the yarns to form a fairly loose, thick ring.

Figure 2

- Thread a tapestry needle with a color of your choice and stitch vertically over this yarn core. Bring the needle and yarn up, over, and behind the core, wrapping tightly.

- Sew around the ring, compressing the wrapped yarn into a bead. The tighter you stitch, the harder and stiffer the bead.

- To change colors and create vertical stripes, drop the first color into the body of the tassel and pick another one from the working group. You can also leave areas unwrapped.

- A knitting needle or thin pencil can be held next to the tassel and the horizontal padding wrapped over it. This allows extra space to insert the needle for the vertical wrapping.

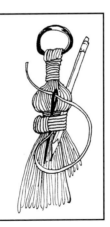

- If your supply of working yarns runs out or if you need another color, just stitch in some extra strands. Yarn beads can be embellished with stitchery or real beads.

Sectional Wrapping

So far we have only discussed wrapping as it applies to the neck, but any area of a tassel can be wrapped.

- For your key ring tassel, try dividing the body (skirt) into at least three sections. Be sure some of the longer working yarns are in each section.

- If you divide the body into a lot of sections, it's easier to work if each section is clipped or loosely knotted to hold that group together while wrapping.

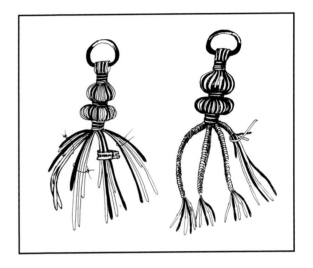

- Wrap each section, then braid or twist them together. Join the groups with a band of wrapping.

Options:

- Leave the wrapped sections as legs.

- Braid, work, or knot the wrapped sections as in a mariner's whisk (see the knot section).

- Divide the yarns into larger or smaller sections and add more braiding or wrapping.

This key ring can go on and on, so now you're on your own. Just remember that it has to fit in your pocket.

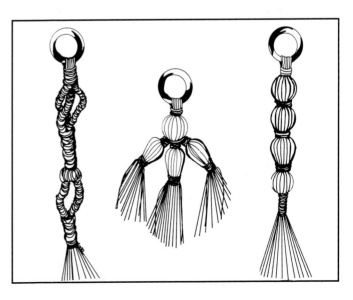

If you really get carried away, you may find yourself with a necklace or belt or even with a dog leash. Key holders make much appreciated gifts, which after all is one "key" to a successful tassel.

Of course tassels aren't limited to key rings. They will adorn anything and everything you can think of! Following are some quickies to speed you along.

ALMOST INSTANT, "NO HASSLE" TASSELS

Most tassels don't take long to make, but here are some super fast ideas:

- Anything with a hole in it can be used to start a tassel. Insert the folded ends of cut yarn through the hole. Pull the cut ends through the loop formed by the fold and—presto!—you have a tassel on a hanger (Fig. 1). Additional yarns can be similarly looped over a cord to create a swag of tassels.

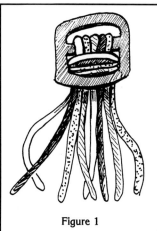

Figure 1

- Take a skein of embroidery floss and fold it in half (or leave it long). Tie a cord through the top and wrap the neck to form a tassel. Just leave the bottom in loops (Fig. 2). This helps keep the ends straight on a garment that will be laundered.

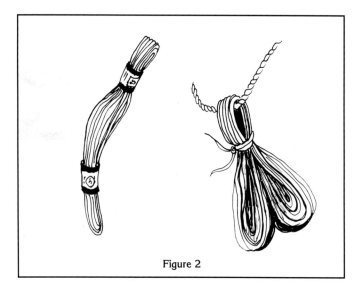

Figure 2

- Make a lightly colored commercial tassel uniquely your own by dipping the end in a pot of dye. The dye will seep up the fiber and create a shaded effect.

- For a bunch of tiny tassels, slit a spool of thread with a razor blade a little bit at a time (Fig. 3). Gather up the threads and tie each bunch at the top. Wrap the neck and trim. These little tassels and the floss tassels can both be used to decorate a larger tassel.

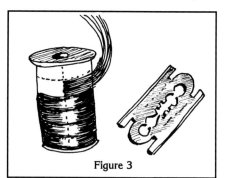

Figure 3

- Tie some yarns together at the top with a cord. Pull the cord through a large-holed bead. Push the bead down over the yarns and trim the ends (Fig. 4, 5).

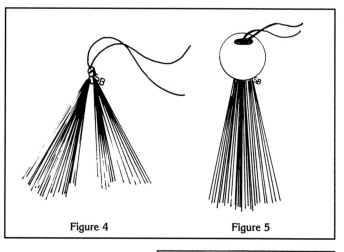

Figure 4   Figure 5

- Tie up a group of yarns, ribbons, or rat-tail cords. Stuff the tied end into a metal bell-cap finding. Add a little glue and crimp the bead shut. For extra glitz, glue sequins or seed beads over the metal cap (Fig. 6).

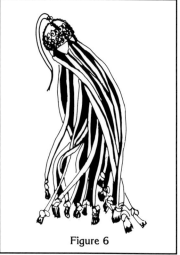

Figure 6

- Roll up commercial ball fringe or bullion fringe to form a tassel. These can be any length from one inch to two feet! Glue or stitch the top to secure (Fig. 7). If the fringe is plied instead of chainette, unwind it for a crinkly look.

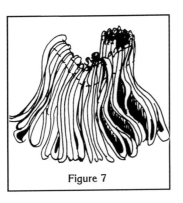

Figure 7

- When making fringe tassels, it's only slightly more trouble to stitch a cord securely to the tape of the fringe before rolling. Then turn the piece upside down, bringing the cord to the outside. The fringe will fall back over the bound area. Smooth it out, wrap the neck, and you'll have a quick tassel with a nice round head (Fig. 8, 9, 10).

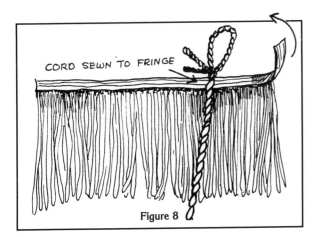

CORD SEWN TO FRINGE

Figure 8

Figure 9

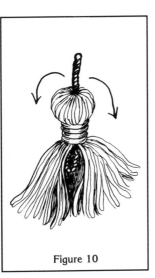

Figure 10

- Make your own fringe by cutting a rectangle of felt, leather, fabric, or ultrasuede; leave one edge uncut. Roll up and glue or stitch the uncut area to form a tassel (Fig. 11).

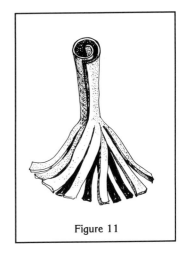

Figure 11

- Tack a string of store-bought seed beads to your tassel for an instant beaded effect.

- You will think of lots of ways to speed up tassel making, but this silly little tassel from Thailand—made by sticking three metallic-paper seals together with a string in the center—is about as simple as any I've seen. Several of these clusters are strung one on top of the other. The bottom seal has a small, crepe paper fringe glued on the end. It makes a wonderful little tassel that sways with every puff of air. You will need three paper seals for each cluster. Fold each seal in half and glue half of one seal to half of another seal. Place the string in the center, glue the third seal to the exposed halves of the other two, and let it sway away (Fig. 12, 13).

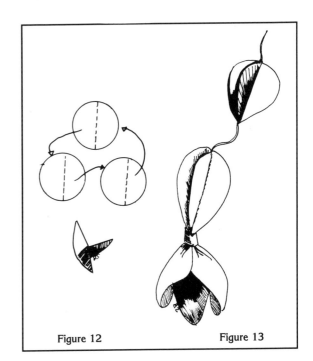

Figure 12   Figure 13

Pompons, Toys, and Ornaments

Written references to tassels are hard to find, but mention of pompons is almost nonexistent. While fashion or home decorating magazines often feature tassels, pompons get almost no press at all (unless a pretty pompon girl is attached). Yet what would American football games be without those colorful pompons? Or skiers without that exclamation point on their caps? Or tennis players minus the pompons on their socks? Or country curtains lacking that fringe of tiny pompons dancing around the hems? And we can't forget clowns with their pompon noses. But in fact, pompons are just fuzzy tassels with their heads hidden in their skirts.

MAKING POMPONS

You can buy plastic disks in assorted sizes for constructing pompons or make your own by cutting two "doughnut" shapes out of cardboard or heavy plastic. A 3" (7.5 cm) disk makes about a 2" (5 cm) pompon. The hole in the middle should be a 1/2" (1.25 cm) to 1" (2.5 cm) in diameter. Don't make it too large.

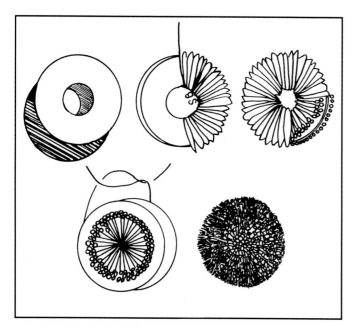

- To form a pompon, place the disks together and wrap yarns radially through the holes and around the outside of both disks until the form is completely covered. Even then it doesn't hurt to thread the yarn and use a needle to fill in the last possible space.

- Pinch the filled circles together in the center and clip around the outside edge to release the outer yarns.

- Tie a very strong yarn or wire between the disks and knot it tightly.

- Remove the disks, trim, and fluff the pompon.

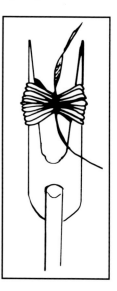

Pompons can also be wound around any two points such as two-pronged kitchen forks, a pair of chopsticks, or two dowels set a few inches apart. As long as a lot of yarn can be wrapped tightly and tied in the middle, it will work. Wrap as much yarn as you can around the form, tie or wire securely in the center, clip the loops, and fluff the pompon. Or for a different look, leave the ends uncut.

Moveable Pompons

To make pompons that will slide on a core or slip over the neck of a tassel, wrap disks as above.

- Then insert the core (a cord, a tassel, or whatever you want the pompon to slide on) through the center hole.

- Clip the yarn around the disk and tie with a strong yarn around the core.

- Remove the disks (Fig. 1).

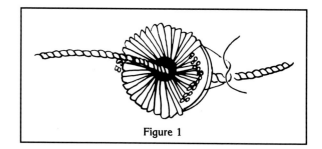

Figure 1

For a variation on the basic pompon:

- Tape a tying thread lengthwise to a dowel or pencil and wrap the pompon yarn over the tying thread.

- Insert the core material (Fig. 2) and slip the wrapped section off the dowel as you tighten the thread. The pompon will spring around the core. Don't cut the

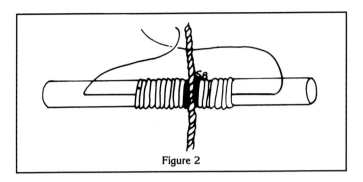

Figure 2

ends. This is a favorite technique in Bolivia, where colorful little pompons are often stacked one on top of the other. Try this on the top of a tassel (Fig. 3).

Production Pompons and Tassels

- The process of making several pompons at one time can be speeded up by winding yarn between two points such as nails in a board, door knobs across from each other, a warping board, etc.

Figure 3

- Tie tightly at regular intervals across all the yarn. To form tassels, leave more space between the ties.

- Clip halfway between the ties.

- Trim and fluff the pompons.

- For a tassel, clip as above, then fold the yarn over at the tie, wrap the neck, and trim the ends.

Mosaic Pompons

You can create quite unusual effects by using the

production winding system and several different colors. Select colors such as green, yellow, and red. Wrap a section of green, then a section of yellow, then red, another yellow, and finally green again. Tie securely, clip, and fluff.

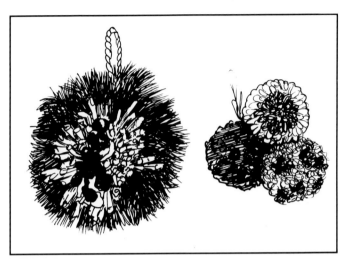

When you get good at this technique, you can make flowers and fancy designs. In Hungary, huge mosaic pompons are assembled into women's hats. The Mien hill-tribe people make them long and striped.

Felted Pompons and Tassels

A wonderful pompon is made in India by forming small fat tassels from dyed, coarse wool fleece. These pudgy tassels are gathered in a circle and massaged in hot, soapy water until the fleece is expanded and felted into a round ball. A quick way to do this at home is to tie each

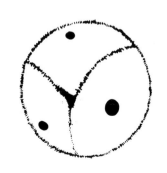

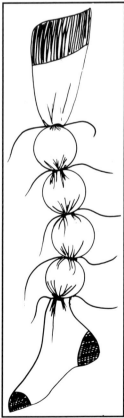

wool pompon in a stocking and leave it in the washing machine through several loads until it becomes firmly felted. (Be sure the wool is colorfast!)

Woven wool cut in strips with tiny seed beads sewn to each strip and felted makes a durable, tangle-proof tassel.

Hard Core Pompons

Wrap a core of rags, yarn, or fleece around a pencil or dowel. (This makes it easier to handle. Remove the pencil when the weaving is complete.) Bind the core material with strong warps to hold it all together and to form a framework for tapestry, coiled basketry, or needleweaving.

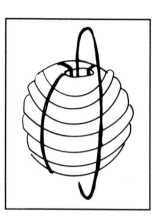

Tapestry Pompons

Wrap a hard core pompon or warp directly on a tassel neck. Weave sections in different colors or stitches to make a tapestry. Use a variety of yarns: metallic, shiny, nubby, etc. When the weaving is complete, use the pompon as is or slip it over tassel yarns to form a head or neck.

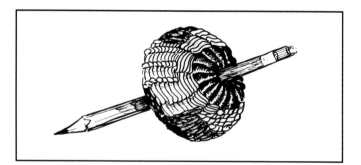

Coiled and Twined Pompons

Denise Hanlon finishes the warp on her exquisite weavings with basketmaking techniques. For her coiled pompons, she starts with a base form which she can stitch onto, like the hard core. By wrapping and coiling a core yarn and then attaching it to the base, she works around the form until it is completely covered, creating a

little basket. A variation is to twine the cover using the core binding as the spokes.

Guatemalan Pompons

The Guatemalans have a unique way of constructing elegant elongated pompons for the ends of slit tapestry sashes. The warp ends are wrapped with heavy string to form a hard core, which may be up to 6" (15 cm) in length. More string is tightly twisted with tufts of yarn inserted between each twist to completely cover the core. The same fiber used in the sash—usually cotton, rayon, or silk—makes up the pompon. The pompon is worked in vertical rows, which allows for the marvelous, striped color changes (see photograph, page 150).

Loose Ends

- Investigate materials: Pompon girls wave paper pompons. Rags and ribbons also can be used.

- The fluffier the yarn, the puffier the pompon.

- Instead of tying with yarn, tie each pompon with wire to hold it securely in place. This is a good technique for decorating a hat or bag with pompons.

- Like multiple tassel groupings, a whole clump of pompons makes a nice arrangement.

TASSEL TOYS AND ORNAMENTS

During World War I, small tassel dolls were used as charms to protect against bombs in Paris and London. For extra luck, they were sometimes attached to horseshoes. Whether you need a lucky charm yourself, or your enthusiasm for tassels has caught on with the younger set, here are some ideas for tassel toys. You can use these little people as they are or add them here and there for a touch of whimsy.

Boy and Girl Tassel Dolls

- Make a regular full tassel and wrap it with a short neck.

- Gather an outer group of yarn on each side to form arms.

- Shorten them slightly and wrap the wrists.

- For a girl tassel, wrap a waist and let the gown flow freely. Embellish her with a beaded necklace, bracelet, or lace collar, etc. A boy tassel is the same as the girl tassel except for the skirt. Wrap the skirt into two leg sections tied at the ankles. Instead of jewelry, try adding a bow tie.

Tassel dolls (Oaxaca, Mexico)

Angel Tassels

To make an angel, start with a white-yarn girl tassel with shiny metallic yarns added. If your yarns are fairly stiff, wrap the "arm" sections at the shoulders, and the angel will have celestial sleeves (Fig. 1). A lace halo

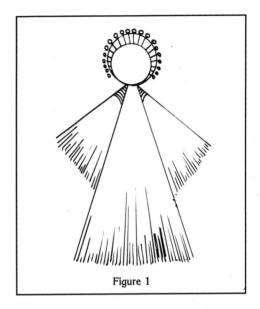

Figure 1

or a small starched doily will complete the look. Add wings of gauze, lace, or silver paper. Hang the angel from a cotton cloud. White satin fabric also can be fashioned tassel-style into an angel. Stuff the head and stitch a face with an angelic smile (Fig. 2).

Figure 2

Santa Claus Tassels

Make a thick boy tassel from red yarn. Tie the waist, wrists, and ankles with black yarn. Glue on a fluff of cotton or felt to make a beard. Add a stocking cap.

Oriental Doll Tassels

Wind a tassel and wrap the neck. Add arms by folding more yarns across the shoulders—kimono style. Bind the extra length to the waist of the original tassel. Stitch features on the face.

Teacher Tassels

Have your child make a doll tassel with a sign that says "My teacher is a doll."

Two-Tone Tassel Figures

Make a figure tassel in one color and wrap a neck. Form arms by winding more yarn in another color and tying near the ends to make wrists. Slip the arms through the tassel yarns under the neck and wrap the waist to secure the arms. Finish with a skirt for a girl or legs for a boy.

Bead Head Tassels

A bead, with or without a painted face, makes a good head for a tassel doll. Fold yarns in half, then tie another yarn around the middle and use it to pull the looped ends up into the bead, leaving the loose ends dangling to form the body. Add hair or a felt hat to the bead.

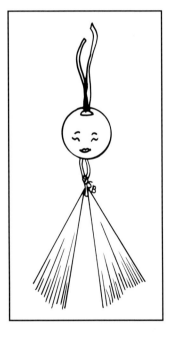

Mexican Folk Tassels

Tiny people tassels dangle from the ends of woven Mexican belts. The warp ends of the belt are used to form the dresses of the girl figures and to pad the bodies of the boy dolls. In both cases, plain white thread is added around the warp ends to form a head, and then the neck is wrapped.

For the girl figure, another group of tassel threads that matches the warps is added just below the neck to make a dress. Separate arms are inserted, the waist is wrapped, and the skirt is clipped. The white portions may be trimmed to form a petticoat or left to hang below the skirt and tied at the ankles to form two legs. On other figures, the colored warp threads form the legs. If the warp contains black thread, the ends of these are used as hair for the doll. Otherwise, separate black threads may be added as a ponytail tassel.

To make the boy doll, the inner warp ends and the outer white portion are wrapped completely to form a chest, which is then divided and wrapped to form the legs. Separate arms are inserted. As a final touch, the faces of both figures are embroidered with eyes and a mouth.

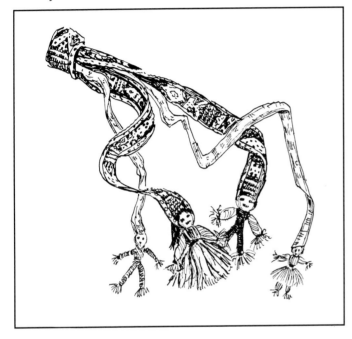

Below: Mexican dolls

Top and bottom right: Tambarin Tassel Doll pins (both made by Lise Lawrence)

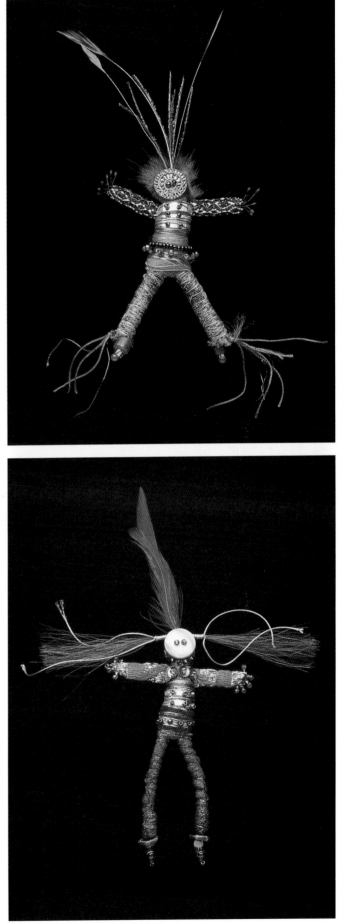

Loose Ends

- The arms of dolls will be neater if you twist the yarns together before binding the wrists.

- If the arms are formed from the body of the tassel instead of separately, be sure to shorten and proportion them before binding the wrists.

- You can insert wires into the arms or body of a doll to create postures. (To be safe, don't use wire if the toy is for a young child.)

- Pipe cleaners or wrapped wires can replace yarn for the arms.

Christmas Ornaments

Tassels make beautiful tree ornaments all by themselves. Use glittery yarns and add lace and beaded necks. Older children enjoy creating fanciful Victorian tassels; these might become family heirlooms. So when 'tis the season, use tassels to decorate your packages, spruce up the gifts, trim the tree, adorn the stockings, and put out with the cookies for Santa.

Christmas Ornaments from the Philippines

Filipino children make star-shaped lanterns called "parols" from lacy, colored foil papers. Candles are placed inside, and fringed paper tassels hang from the points. These lanterns traditionally hang over the nativity scene and are carried throughout the villages on Christmas Eve (Fig. 1).

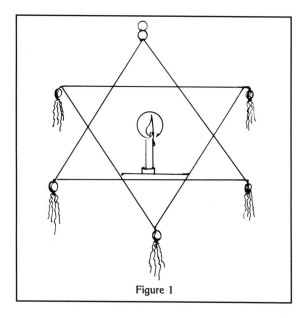

Figure 1

The tassels are formed by folding a rectangle of tissue paper in half and fringing the ends. The paper is then opened, and the uncut area is scrunched up to form the head. The paper is again folded in half, and the neck is wired. One end of the wire is pushed up through the head to make a hanger (Fig. 2, 3).

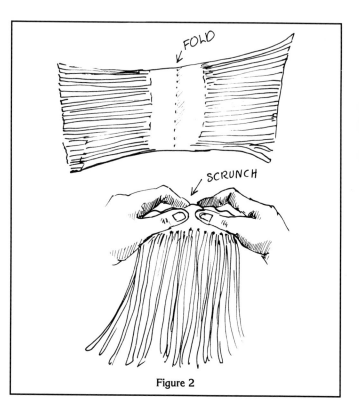

Figure 2

Figure 3

Another Filipino ornament is made by attaching a simple tassel to a glittery, decorative top. The tassel is made by cutting a design in a square of paper or plastic. The pierced design forms the head and is placed over a fringed piece of paper attached to a stiffer paper ring (Fig. 4, 5, 6).

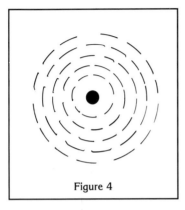

Figure 4

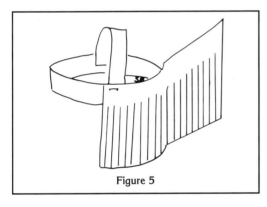

Figure 5

Figure 6

Pumpkin Pompons

For another holiday decoration, make a bunch of fat orange pompons. Cut facial features from black felt and glue them on, or embroider fanciful expressions.

Kitty Toys

You've taken care of the kids; now how about the kitties? Cats have an affinity for yarn, so why not give your felines a treat? (Do be careful, however, not to let your cat swallow long pieces of yarn; these can cause serious problems). Make a fluffy (but sturdy) yarn pompon. Hang it on a long cord from the back of your chair. Or stuff a yarn tassel with catnip, cut the skirt very short, and add a long yarn tail; it's guaranteed to drive cats nuts. You could make the tassel mouse-shaped, but the cat will love it just as it is.

While my illustrator Gail was working on this book with me, Parker—her little Scottie—felt neglected, so we paused to make him a doggie tassel.

Gentle Giant Ball Pompon

I invented this oversized pompon from very thick, soft yarn because I live in a glass house, and my grandsons—Sam and Tanner—like to throw things at each other. They're only three and four, so their aim is still less than perfect! Both boys love the gigantic ball—the soft fibers make it easy for little fingers to catch—and I'm happy not having to duck every time they heave off with a pass.

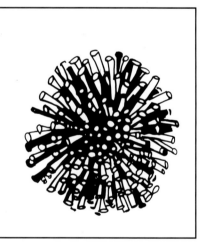

Granny Necklace

Grannies should have some fun too. Try stringing an assortment of little boy and girl, angel, and Santa Claus tassels on a pretty cord or colorful shoelace to create this whimsical necklace.

And speaking of grannies, Gail saw a pair of old-fashioned glasses at an antique show. The ear pieces weren't curved, so tassel-weighted cords had been added to keep the glasses on. A practical use for tassels at last!

Whether you make key holders, toys, pompons, or just plain tassels, the key is simply to have fun creating them.

Above: Granny necklace

Below: Tassels for eyeglasses

All the Trimmings

Tassels gain much of their charm from the infinite variety of hanging cords, braids, and decorative knots that can be added to them. In this chapter, we will consider some of the possibilities for embellishing and personalizing your tassels.

Left: Individual wool braids are looped in half to form the skirts for three of these tassels. The other two tassels are made from loops of twisted cotton string. The ends of the wool braids are enclosed with a tiny, circular wool tassel; the string ends have been dipped in pitch. Metal caps and beads are used as spacers.

Right: Finger-woven braids form the holding cords for this tassel from Ladakh. Buttonhole rings, circles of seed beads, and buttons decorate the braid before the twenty-two strands are divided into needlewoven sections. Finally, small bullion fringe tassels with seed beads at the end and needlelace heads are added.

The diamond design on this braided llama collar from Peru is made with thirty-two strands of wool.

Braided door decoration with pompons and wrapping (Morocco)

The way you choose to hang a tassel depends on its final use. How long a hanger do you need? Will it receive a lot of wear? Is the hanger the most prominent part of the tassel (as in a bell pull)? Once you have assembled all the threads and yarns for your tassel, pause and consider the most appropriate way to attach or hang it. Besides its use, consider proportion, color, and balance. You wouldn't want to dangle an elegant tassel from a limp string or have the cord come off after the first tug.

The weight of yarn determines the size and body of the cord. A thicker hanger can be made using many threads in place of a single strand. Braids can be worked over a core for even more bulk. Try using two or more colors or a variegated yarn to form cords or braids. Just be sure they don't get so elaborate that they outshine the tassel.

Hangers are an integral part of many tassels. Most require no tools, just your hands for stranded braids or fingers for slentre braids and finger crochet, but by adding simple tools such as a rope maker, additional effects are easily created.

The techniques for making hangers that you're about to learn range from simple to fairly complex. All these hangers can be added to the tassel in the same way as the short cord described in the last chapter, or they can be doubled over to form a looped hanger.

Other possibilities not discussed here involve more equipment and skill. You'll find references for sling braid-ing (used extensively in Peru) and kumihimo braiding (a Japanese favorite) at the end of this section.

CORDS

Earlier, we made a simple finger-twisted cord. Sometimes this won't be long enough or fast enough to suit your needs.

Long Twisted Cords

To make a longer cord, you'll need a loop of yarn or yarns about five times the intended finished length (just as you needed for a short cord).

- After forming the loop, slip one end over a hook or door knob and put a pencil in the other end of the loop.

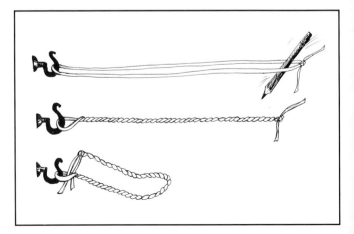

- Pull taut and twirl the pencil until the yarns kink. Test by releasing the tension slightly. Stop when the yarn twists back on itself. Overtwisting gives a firmer, harder cord.

- Double the cord back on itself carefully to form a smooth, even hanger.

- Knot the ends together to prevent them from untwisting.

Speedy Twisted Cords

Cord making can be speeded up by using an electric hand mixer or drill to do the twisting.

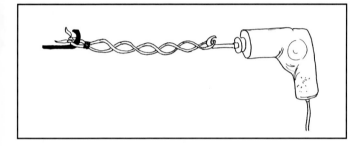

- Attach one end of the loop to a sturdy hook and secure the loop with a rubber band so it won't bounce off.

- Attach the other end of the loop to the drill and turn it on for a second to twist thoroughly.

- Fold the cord in half and secure the ends.

If you have a sewing machine, the bobbin winder can be used in the same manner to twist lightweight cords. Slip one end of the loop around the bobbin and through the top hole to secure it. Then put your finger or a pencil in the other end of the loop and turn on the machine. If you have a friend hold the end, you can make the cord as long as you like. Otherwise you are limited to the distance you can reach from the machine's controls (a great stretching exercise).

Cords Twisted on a Rope Maker

The rope machine—invented by Leonardo da Vinci—makes it easy to produce a long thick cord because the yarn is not doubled back on itself. Instead, it's twisted in one direction, then transferred and twisted in the opposite direction. You can buy or make a rope machine (Fig. 1).

To make one, you'll need three heavy wire coat hangers, strong pliers, and two smooth 3/4" (1.875 cm) thick boards about 15" (37.5 cm) long and 4" (10 cm) wide.

- Hold the two boards together and drill a 1/8" (.3125 cm) diameter hole through the center of both boards.

- Then drill holes about 4-1/2" (11.25 cm) from either side of the center hole. The holes must line up exactly through the two boards.

- Next, cut three 8" (20 cm) long straight sections of wire from the coat hangers.

- Bend about 1" (2.5 cm) on one end of each section

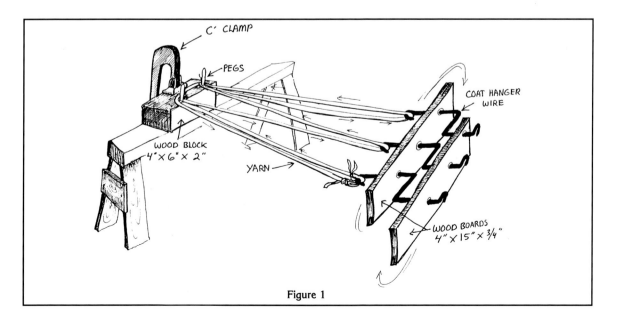

Figure 1

to make little loops. Insert the other ends through the holes on one board.

- Hold the loops snug against the board and bend the long wires at ninety-degree angles so they are parallel with the board.

- About 2-1/2" (6.25 cm) from these bends, make another ninety-degree bend in each wire so that the long ends will pass through the holes in the second board. In each wire, the bend must be exactly the same distance from the previous bend.

- When all the wires are bent, thread them through the second board.

- Then, bend hooks in the end of each wire to hold the yarn. Set this aside.

- Make a yarn separator to hold the other ends of the yarn. Get a small wooden block about 2" by 3" (5 by 7.5 cm), drill holes in it, and insert two 3" (7.5 cm) long dowels about 1" (2.5 cm) apart.

If all this sounds too complicated, you'll find a commercial rope machine listed among the resources at the end of this section. Whether you use a commercial product or make your own, the following rope making instructions apply.

- Clamp the yarn separator pegs to a table or whatever is convenient for the length rope you want to make.

- Set the rope winder at a distance slightly farther away than the length of the finished rope. Brace it on a chair or have a friend hold it. For example, to make a 3 ft. (90 cm) rope, move the rope winder a little over 3 ft. (90 cm) from the pegs. There will be a small amount of take-up, depending on the thickness of the yarn you are using and how tightly you twist the rope, so this is an approximate distance.

- The yarn will be strung between the winder and the pegs. Tie the yarn to the first hook of the winder.

- Then take it around the outside of the first peg and back up to the second hook on the winder.

- Loop the yarn over the hook and carry it back around the inside of the second peg and back to the third hook on the winder. Loop over this hook and then take the yarn back around both pegs and back up to the first hook on the winder.

- There should now be a loop of yarn (two rows) on each hook. This is enough to form a rope, but you can repeat the procedure to make a thicker piece. Cut the yarn end and make it into a loop to slip over the first hook that holds the starting loop.

- To make the rope, hold the winder in the center of the outer board (Fig. 2).

- Crank in a clockwise direction with one hand while holding the board with the hooks and yarn steady

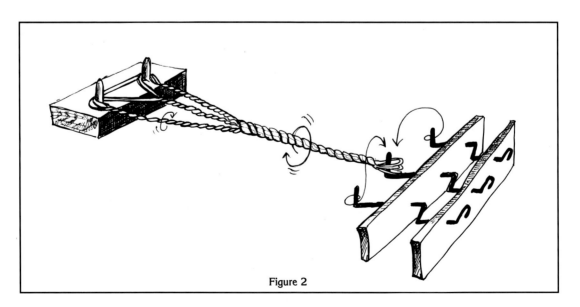

Figure 2

with your other hand. Crank away until the yarn is tightly twisted; the more you twist the tighter the rope will be.

- When you are satisfied, transfer the yarns from each outer hook to the center hook, carefully keeping the yarn taut (Fig. 2, page 84).

- Twist in the opposite direction to form the rope.

- Remove the finished rope from the pegs and the center hook, tie knots in all ends, and admire this amazing accomplishment.

Three separate ropes can be formed and then put on the machine and rewound to produce an even more amazing rope. Just keep alternating the direction of the twist. Most formal tassel cords are wound this way, but on a much more complicated machine.

Commercial rope machines operate on the same principle. Fibers are twisted left to right (clockwise) to spin yarn; this is called a "Z" twist. Yarns are twisted right to left (counterclockwise) for an "S" twist. You can look at yarn and see the angle of the twist that has been spun into it. It will veer to the left like an "S" or to the right like a "Z". Check by twisting the yarn; a twist to the right will unply an "S" yarn and will make a "Z" yarn tighter.

This is important to know because you need to twist yarns in the opposite direction to ply them together (Fig. 3).

Finger Crocheted Cords

Finger crochet uses a single strand of yarn. I've also seen this technique referred to as "monkey chain" and "an idiot's delight." (Does that tell you anything?) You work from the center of a strand, alternating loops between index fingers. For a fancier effect, tie two different colored strands together at the beginning, or pre-string beads on the cord and move them into position as you work.

- To start, fold a single cord in half or tie two colors together.

- Make a slip loop on your right index finger.

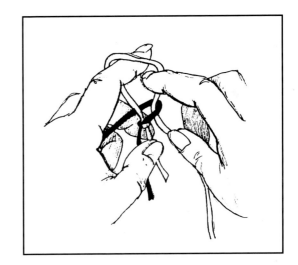

- Slide your left index finger alongside your right finger, through the loop, and pick up a loop from the other half of the cord. Pull it through and remove your right finger.

Figure 3

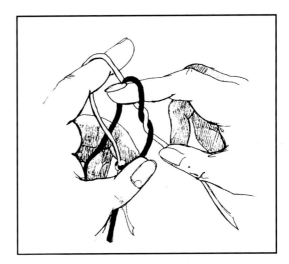

• With your right hand, pull down on the end of the first loop to tighten the cord.

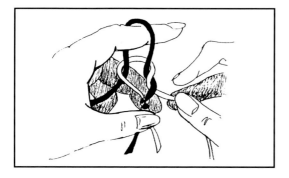

• Repeat the process by picking up another loop with your right finger and tightening with your left hand. Control the tension on the working ends with the little finger of each hand.

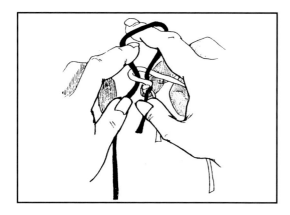

• Alternate index fingers to pull the yarn through the loop, first from one side and then from the other. Tighten after each pass by pulling down on the cord as it forms with the thumb and index finger of the hand not holding the active loop.

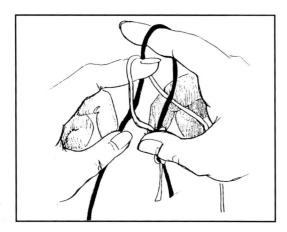

• When you reach the end, pull the loose end through the last loop and tighten to secure.

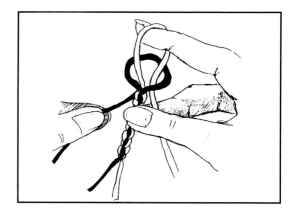

Some people find it easier to switch fingers (as shown in the diagram), but it isn't necessary.

Of course you can also use a crochet hook to make a cord. A nice rounded cord results from using a triple-chain foundation. Single crochet back on this chain, then slip stitch the third row.

Shirred Cords

For an extra-special look, try making a shirred cord. Sew a tube of velvet or satin fabric and squish it over a rope or other cord material. It should be loose and wrinkled. Turn the ends under and attach it to your most extraordinary tassel.

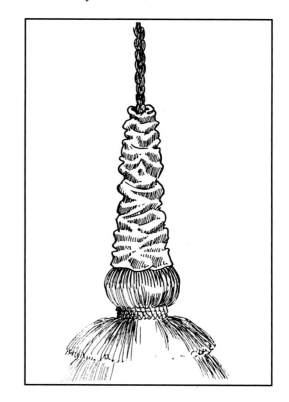

BRAIDS

Because textiles deteriorate over time and clay does not, most early evidence of braiding comes from pressed designs found in pottery. Japanese ceramics from as early as 3000 B.C. show braid patterns. Braids evolved to produce a sturdier and more decorative surface structure than cords.

If twisting isn't your style, an endless variety of flat and round braids can be used as hanging cords. A clipboard makes a handy holder and tensioner for the yarn ends as you work, as do masking tape or pins. People from many cultures, however, simply use the big toe. A nice finished edge is made by looping strands (using a lark's head knot) across the top of a long strand; the longer strand then becomes the outside pair of the braiding group.

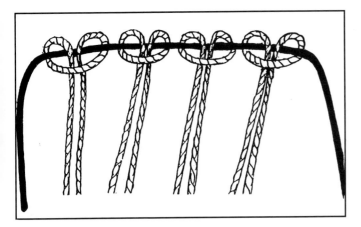

Uniform tension is necessary for smooth, crisp braids, although the character of a braid can easily be changed by pulling on one of the strands as you work.

Three-Strand Distorted Braids

Try a three-strand braid with one dark and two light strands. Braid a few inches and pull on the dark strand. Braid some more and pull again. If all your yarns are one color, tie a small knot in the end of one strand to remind you of which one to pull. You'll probably want to be consistent. There are two sides to this braid. Play with it until you get the distorted effect you like.

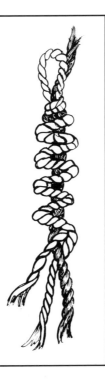

Four-Strand Braids

Once you master the rhythm, these go very quickly. Use two colors in pairs to form patterns or four different colors for a lively effect.

Four-Strand Round Braids

Although there are variations, this is an easy one because it's essentially a three-strand pigtail alternating from side to side. Work with three on one side, then three on the other side while the opposite outside strand takes a rest. Work back to front or front to back, whichever is easier for you:

- Back to Front: The outside strand goes under two, around the third, and drops between strands two and three. Strands one and two are always on left side. Strands three and four are always on right side.

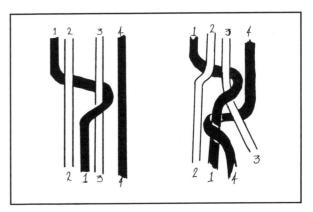

- Front to Back: Bring first strand over two center

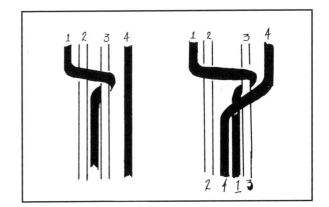

strands and under the center right strand. Then bring right strand over two center strands and under center left.

Flat Braids

Spiral Braids: When set up with 1 and 4 as dark strands and 2 and 3 as light strands, the colors alternate from side to side and a spiral pattern is formed:

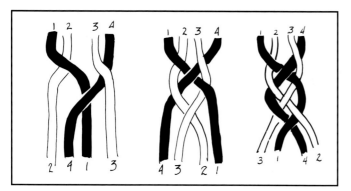

- Outside 1 passes over strand 2.

- Strand 4 passes behind 3 and over 1.

- Strand 2, which is now the outside left, crosses over 4 only.

- Strand 3, which is now outside right, passes behind and next to strand 1 and over 2, which is the next one.

Sequence: left strand over; right strand behind, then over; repeat.

Chevron Braids: Worked in two colors, the strands cross in the center forming a chevron as the colors alternate down the length of the braid. When you use eight strands— four dark and four light—an "M" pattern develops.

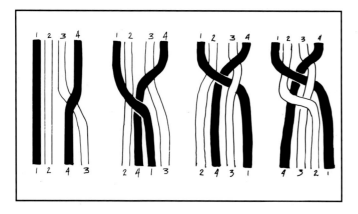

Sequence for four strands: First, outside strands cross over inner pair, then inner set becomes outer pair, crosses to center, and switches position with left strand on top.

Braid Drafting System

Clotilde V. Barrett showed me her concise braid drafting system, which saves drawing a lot of diagrams. Here's how it works:

- The "X" indicates the working strand.

- The solid squares show that the working strand goes over those warps.

- The working strand goes under the squares with the dot.

- The working strand starts by going behind (under) all the squares.

Notice how this system applies to the six-strand round braid.

Six (or More) Strand Round Braids

Round braids with any even number of strands follow the same sequence. Secure the stationary ends of the braids (by pinning or clipping) before proceeding. It takes a few passes to get the braid started and under control.

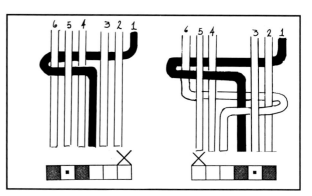

Sequence:

- The right strand 1 goes behind all the other strands, then turns and weaves over, under, over to the center.

- Then the left-hand strand 6 goes behind all the strands, turns, and goes over, under, and finally over the original strand 1.

- Repeat these two steps, taking the outside strands and working them to the middle each time. (In this case, you'd move strands 2 and 5 next.)

Braids with any even number of strands will produce a round, square, half-round, or spiral braid if you follow these charts.

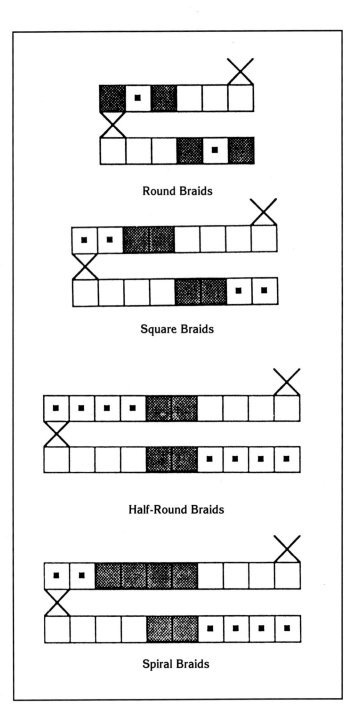

Round Braids

Square Braids

Half-Round Braids

Spiral Braids

For braids with an odd number of strands, follow these sequences to produce shaped braids.

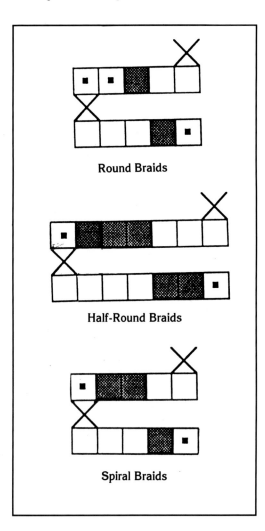

Round Braids

Half-Round Braids

Spiral Braids

Braids Worked Over a Core

A thicker, heavier cord can be made by working braids over an inner core of yarn, jute, or rope. Adding a strand of wire will allow the finished piece to be shaped.

- Position the core in the center of the braiding material.

- Work the braid around it, always encasing the core. (Sometimes it helps to pin the core at the top and bottom so it doesn't flop around.)

- Any number of core strands can be used to obtain the desired thickness; the core is simply the silent partner.

- You can leave the core to give structure to the braid, or you can remove it to produce a hollow cord. The tassel ends can then be pulled up into the hollow cord.

Needlewoven Braids

Needleweaving over a two-strand core produces a neat, bound braid.

- Loop the covering yarn in a figure eight over the core. Pack it tightly for a secure finish.

- Change colors as you go along, laying the unused colors next to the core and working over them. Pick up the colors as needed.

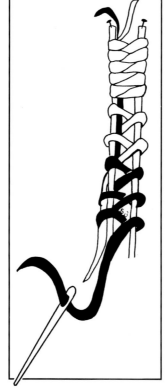

- Any number of core strands, divided into sections, can be used for needleweaving. Pin them down to form warps and weave in and out with a threaded tapestry needle.

- The resulting braid can be doubled to form a looped holding cord or left flat to form the top of the tassel.

- A wide needlewoven piece can be rounded and stuffed to make an interesting tassel head.

Slentre Braids

If you like to let your fingers do the walking, try slentre, which is Danish for stroll or saunter. It's called "puncetto" work in the Italian Alps, where it's used as a finish on lace collars and cuffs. Braids are worked with

loops on your fingers, which avoids tangled ends.

This technique is best for short braids because you have to open your arms wide to pull the twists tight and to maintain an even tension; the length of the braid is limited to the spread of your arms. A longer braid can be made, however, by retying the ends every two feet.

The take-up is about half, so 24" (60 cm) loops will give you approximately 12" (30 cm) of finished braid, depending on the thickness of your yarn and how tightly it is pulled.

Both hands and five loops are used in this technique; your fingers "stroll" as the index finger of one hand is inserted through a loop on the opposite hand in order to hook a loop and pull it back to the first side. The process is then repeated in the reverse direction, moving the loops over to free the index finger. The shape of the braid is determined by which side of the loop is hooked and transferred, and by which loop it is pulled through.

Palms can face up or down; the index fingers do the work. (Laotians make the same braids with the palms facing each other while the pick-up is done with the ring fingers. I prefer to work palms down with the fingers downward through the loops.)

Whether you are making a half-round, flat, spiral, or squared braid, you will need five equal loops of sturdy yarn (pearl cotton works well).

- To prepare for any of these four patterns, cut five lengths and tie an overhand knot in each length to form a loop.

- Tie all the loops together at the knotted end.

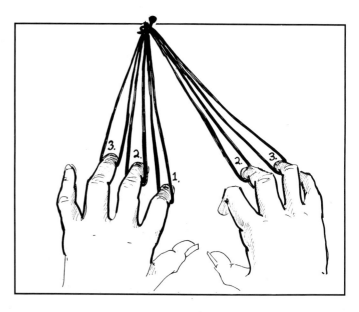

• Fasten the bundle of knotted ends to a stationary object. The Indians of South America use their big toe. I use a clipboard, but any hook, nail, or doorknob will do.

• To begin, put a loop on the three middle fingers of your left hand and a loop on the ring finger and the middle finger of your right hand. Hook your fingers slightly so the loops don't fall off. (With the palms and fingers pointing up, you turn your hand over as you do the pick-up. The directions are the same as long as the index finger is always number 1.)

As you read the instructions below, refer to the diagrams and the technique should become clear. The pairs of circles represent the two strands of each yarn loop. The dark line is the route the index finger (X) takes to hook one side of the loop on the third finger and return it to the opposite hand.

Half-Round Braids

To create a half-round braid:

• Move your right index finger through the loop held by finger 2 on the left hand and hook the inner strand of the loop held by finger 3 on the left hand.

• Lift it up, pull it through the loop on finger 2, and transfer the entire loop to the right index finger 1.

• Shift the remaining two loops on the left hand over so they are on fingers 3 and 2, leaving the left index finger free.

• Repeat the same procedure on the right side. That is: the left index finger 1 goes down into the loop on right side finger 2, pulls the inner strand of the loop on finger 3 through loop 2, and transfers it to the left index finger 1. Again, shift the remaining loops over to free the right index finger.

• Separate your hands outward to tighten the braid up to the holding knot after each pass. The left-hand cords go to the left side and right-hand cords separate to the right side.

• Repeat from side to side until the loops are completely and evenly braided.

It takes a few passes for the braid to start developing. Keep the tension as even as possible on all the loops, and remember to pull your hands apart to tighten the braid as you work.

(continued on page 94)

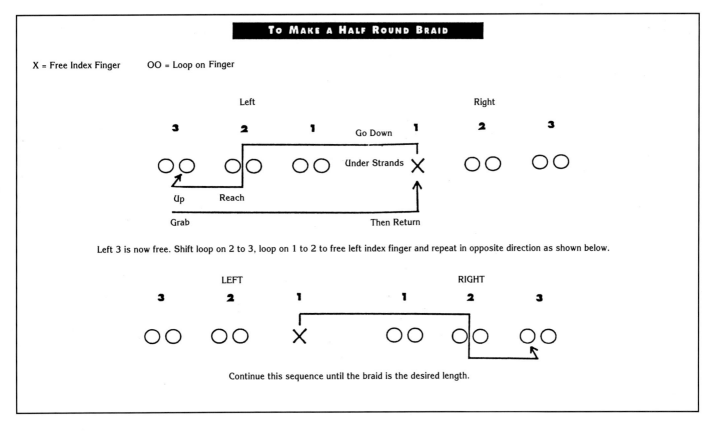

TO MAKE A HALF ROUND BRAID

X = Free Index Finger   OO = Loop on Finger

Left   Right

3   2   1   Go Down   1   2   3

Under Strands   X

Up   Reach

Grab   Then Return

Left 3 is now free. Shift loop on 2 to 3, loop on 1 to 2 to free left index finger and repeat in opposite direction as shown below.

LEFT   RIGHT

3   2   1   1   2   3

X

Continue this sequence until the braid is the desired length.

Tassels: The Fanciful Embellishment

Opposite page, upper left: An interesting series of tassels are layered on the braid of this "wichi-wichi" (ceremonial dance tassel) from Cuzco, Peru.

Opposite page, upper right: Neckpieces made with a Mien version of slentre braiding are available from the Laotian Handcraft Center.

Opposite page, lower left: Afghan camel bag

Opposite page, lower right: Two-tiered braided and knotted tassel

Left: An Indonesian man

Below: Colorfully braided hair

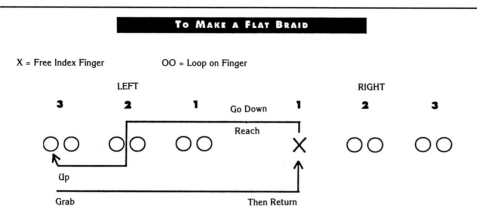

TO MAKE A FLAT BRAID

X = Free Index Finger   OO = Loop on Finger

LEFT   RIGHT
3   2   1   Go Down   1   2   3

Reach

X

Go Down / Reach / Up / Grab / Then Return

Left 3 is now free. Shift loop on 2 to 3, loop on 1 to 2 to free left index finger and repeat in opposite direction as shown below.

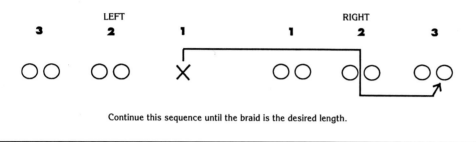

LEFT   RIGHT
3   2   1   1   2   3

X

Continue this sequence until the braid is the desired length.

(continued from page 91)
Flat Braids

Use the same system for a flat braid, but this time hook the outer part of the loop on the third finger at each pass.

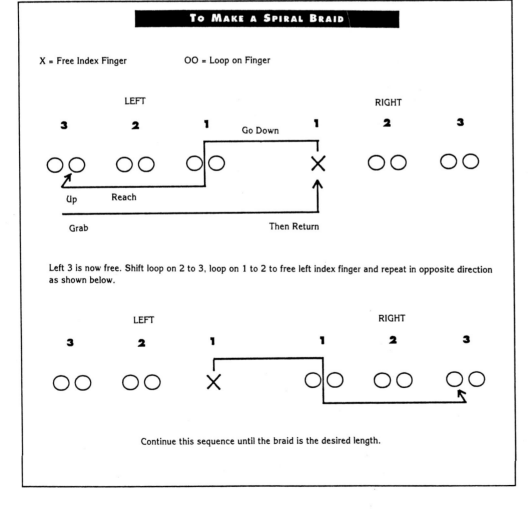

TO MAKE A SPIRAL BRAID

X = Free Index Finger   OO = Loop on Finger

LEFT   RIGHT
3   2   1   Go Down   1   2   3

X

Up / Reach / Grab / Then Return

Left 3 is now free. Shift loop on 2 to 3, loop on 1 to 2 to free left index finger and repeat in opposite direction as shown below.

LEFT   RIGHT
3   2   1   1   2   3

X

Continue this sequence until the braid is the desired length.

Spiral Slentre Braids

For a spiral braid, the right index finger goes through the loop on the left index finger, under the loop on the left middle finger, and then grasps the inner strand of the loop on the third finger and pulls it through to the right side. Transfer the loops on the left hand to free the left index finger and repeat from left to right. Work back and forth as before.

94   *Tassels: The Fanciful Embellishment*

Squared Braids

For a squared braid, you must reach down through the index finger loop, up between it and the next loop, then down again through the middle finger loop. Pull the inner strand of the far loop through both the middle finger loop and the index finger loop. Proceed as in the other braids.

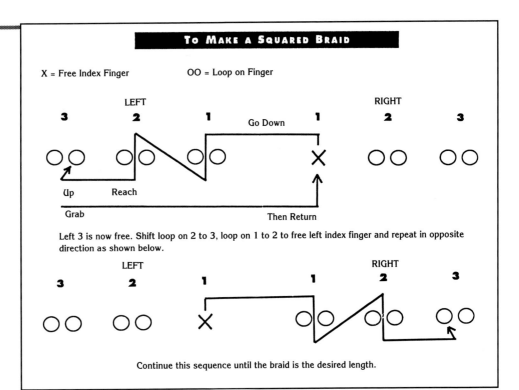

X = Free Index Finger   OO = Loop on Finger

LEFT   RIGHT
3   2   1   Go Down   1   2   3

Up   Reach
Grab   Then Return

Left 3 is now free. Shift loop on 2 to 3, loop on 1 to 2 to free left index finger and repeat in opposite direction as shown below.

LEFT   RIGHT
3   2   1   1   2   3

Continue this sequence until the braid is the desired length.

Loose Ends

- Try using different colored loops or tie one light and one dark yarn together to form a loop. The color that shows on the braid front is determined by which side of the loop is picked up. Variegated yarns also work well for this.

- Squared braids are particularly interesting when made in two colors.

- Slentre braids work up quickly and make nice friendship bracelets.

Flat Woven Braided Tassels

You may fall in love with making braids and forget that you started out to create a tassel holder. If so, you'll find that most flat woven braids can simply form the tassel. To make the braid as a hanger, measure half the number of yarns, twice as long as needed, and fold them in the center to give a finished top edge. Pin or clip to a board for braiding.

To use the braid as a head for a tassel, start the braiding in the center area of your tassel yarns, leaving the top and bottom ends to form the skirt. (Masking tape works well to secure this one.) The braid can be left flat and the bottom stitched to secure the braiding, or it can be wrapped. Add additional yarns for a fuller skirt.

Here are two braids you can use to dress up your tassels. I chose these because I like the names Ester Dendel gave them:

Lights in the Window at Night

This is a twelve-strand braid, with six light and six dark strands. If you plan to make the braid itself into a tassel (rather than adding a skirt later), it's best to use a clump of fine threads to form each strand. That way the skirt of the tassel will have more body.

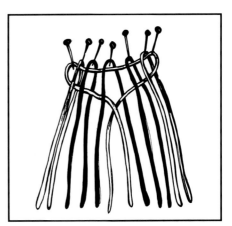

- The six, dark-colored strands start in the middle with three light strands on each side.

- Beginning with the first, right-hand light strand, weave over one, under one, over, under, and over to the center. The light strand is now in the center and held in the left hand.

- The next pass is made by using the light strand on the left-hand side and weaving to the center. Start by going under, then over, under, over, and under to the center to join the right-hand group of threads.

- Continue working the outside strands to the center (where they switch sides) until the braid or head of your tassel is the desired length (and the lights are in the window).

Cows in a Pen

To make this braid, use twelve light strands (or clumps of threads) in the center with three dark strands on each side for a total of eighteen strands.

- The weaving starts on the right side, going over two, under two, over two, and under two to the center, where it joins with the left-hand group of threads.

- The left outside strand is then woven over two, under two, and over two to the center, where it will go under three (two of the light strands and the new dark strand) and join the right-hand group of threads.

This is repeated to form a pattern where all the light and dark threads (cows) are captured in the center (pen). Obviously, switching the colors gives a different effect.

Attaching Braids to Tassels

Tassels can be put anywhere on a braid (Fig. 1). To use them on the end, pull the tassel yarns through the last section of braid or tie a knot and join the braid to a tassel the same way we did with the cord in the special-

key holder (Fig. 2). Or leave a tail of unbraided yarns to become the skirt and then wrap to form a tassel head. Tassel yarns can be worked in as the braid is formed or pulled through afterwards. Wrapping the neck secures the tassel to the braid (Fig. 3).

Figure 2

Figure 1

Figure 3

More Loose Ends

- Braids can be started in the center of the lengths of yarn and folded over to form a loop. This provides twice the number of ends for the skirt. Or double the braid in the center, wrap a neck, and unbraid the ends to form the tassel.

- As a rule of thumb, make the strands about 1-1/2 times the finished length. I always add a little bit more to be safe and gain a longer fringe. If you do run short on a piece, you can splice a new strand to the old one by unraveling each strand and twisting the two together. Add a drop of glue if necessary.

- Another way to add a new strand is to lay it along-side the original strand and cut the two at an angle to eliminate bulk. Overlap and work the two strands together for a few inches. It's best to add new ones at the center of the braid.

- When weaving tabby (over one, under one) with an even number of strands that are woven from both sides, one side must start by weaving over and the opposite side must start by weaving under the first warp strand.

- Flat braids terminating in a fringe are used for belts and for the Japanese obi-jimo cord that secures and accents the obi (belt) on a kimono. A tassel is formed by wrapping the bottom of the braid.

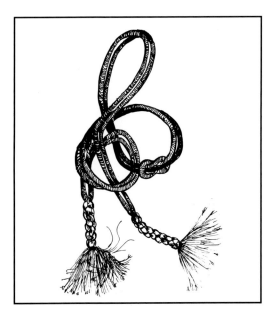

- Another word for a braid is "gimp."

Things to Do With Braids and Cords

- Decorate the cord by beading, sewing on buttons (perhaps with beaded thread), or by adding charms, amulets, dangles, or even more tassels.

- Try dividing the braid and wrapping it in sections.

- Wrap sections of the cord and then form the sections into a mat knot. Use a tassel to hide the separation. Keep braiding, and when you run out of cord, use tassels at its ends.

- Beads and trinkets can be sewn on after the cord is complete or strung on a strand as the braid is being made.

- Loop braids and cords to form a frog, then add a rosette in the center and tassels on the end.

- Use braids or ropes as the tassel body. Double the length and gather them together to form the tassel. Wrap the neck and leave them as is or free the ends.

- Use braids to add feathers or other dangles to a tassel. Braid the neck or wrap it with braids.

In this section, we've only hinted at the possible ways to "tie one on." Other hanging devices for tassels can be found in books on braiding. These are some I have used:

- *Basic Book of Finger Weaving*, by Ester Dendel, Simon & Schuster, 1974.

- *Braiding and Knotting: Techniques and Projects*, by Constantine Belash, Dover Publications.

- *African Fabric Crafts*, by Ester Dendel, Taplinger Publishing Co., 1974.

- *Sling Braiding of the Andes*, by Adele Cahlender (available from Dos Tenedora, 3036 N. Snelling, St. Paul, MN 55113)

- *Kumi Himo in Japan*, by Hoko Tokoro, Ogaki Unesco Association, Japan, 1983.

The incredible rope machine may be available at your local weaving shop. (Always check there first. If we don't support local suppliers, there won't be any local suppliers left.) One manufacturer is the Schacht Spindle Company, 6101 Ben Place, Boulder, Colorado 80301.

Knotted and tasseled hair ornaments (India)

Top It Off! Knots

"**I**n knot making one feels as when kneeling in deep reverence before one's great master. Perhaps this creative tension is what the secret charm of knot making is all about." So says Mrs. Kim Hee-Jin, founder and president of the Korean Maedup (art of knotting) Institute. I agree that certain knots make me feel very humble (or stupid). Perhaps more concentration on the secret charm would help. Knots are an integral part of most Oriental tassels, and some knowledge of knot tying will prove helpful in tassel construction.

Ancient bone needles and ceramic spindles provide evidence that the Koreans have practiced knotting as an art form since prehistoric times. The earliest knotted pieces found date from 108 B.C.

Knots can be used on the holding cord of the tassel, as a head for a tassel, or as an embellishment on the tassel itself. Some knots work all three ways, depending on how they are pulled and finished. A turk's head knot, for instance, may encircle the holding cord, form the head of the tassel, or serve as a flat decoration.

To practice knot making, it's easiest to start with a firm but flexible material such as a braided nylon cord. A knot may be formed with a single cord or with a clump of yarns treated as a single cord. The latter is used when making a knot to form the head of a tassel. Even when the diagrams show a single cord, the yarns that form the tassel can be divided into sections and each section worked as a single element. The knot will be easier to maneuver if the sections are long and slim.

Knot names are confusing. I have tried to use nautical terminology, but even sailors don't always agree on the same name. Sometimes there is a "sequence" listed at the end of each knot. This is my litany for weaving in the ends; I hope it proves helpful. The diagrams may be all you need.

A word of warning: Knots, like braids, can become a life's work. The books listed at the end of this chapter could keep you busy for years. *The Ashley Book of Knots* has over 3,500 entries. Not all the knots I have chosen are traditional to tassels, but they all make unusual or unique additions to your creations.

KNOTS FORMED ON THE HOLDING CORD

These knots—often referred to as "mat" or "flat" knots—frequently decorate Chinese pendant tassels.

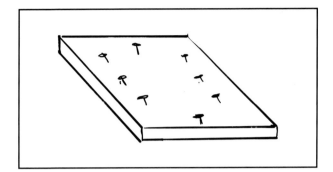

Long straight pins or T pins will help to maintain the shape of curves and to keep your place as you work. If you plan on reproducing the same shape several times, a pattern-tying jig can be constructed using pins in Cellotex board, nails in a wooden board, or any system you can devise to create an even and consistent spacing.

Some designs are started at one end of the cord and others are started in the middle. (The latter are referred to as on the "bight" or bend in the cord.) The way you pull the completed knot determines how it will work.

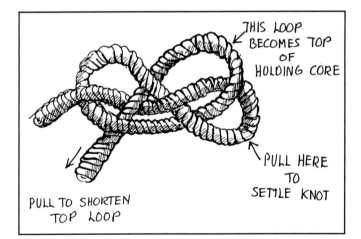

PULL TO SHORTEN TOP LOOP

THIS LOOP BECOMES TOP OF HOLDING CORE

PULL HERE TO SETTLE KNOT

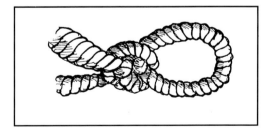

Play with it, manipulate it in various ways, and see what happens. Look at both sides and twist it in several directions. You may like it flat on the holding cord or as the head of a tassel.

Carrick Bend on a Bight

This easy knot—one of the many referred to as a "Chinese" knot—is made with a single cord or with a group of yarns used as a single cord. It's the beginning of a turk's head knot, and the use is not limited to the holding cord.

• Start by pinning the center of the cord at the top.

• Then cross the left end over the right to form a loop for the top.

• Using the same end, form a loop on the right side.

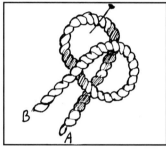

• Pick up the original right-hand end A and bring it up and over the other end B to form a loop on the left side. At this point none of the strands are interlaced. They just lay across each other.

• Weave the end A under the left side of the top loop.

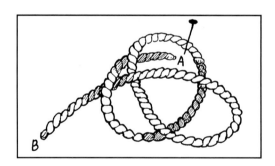

• Weave end A over the left strand B, which is now in the middle of the loop, under the right side of the top loop, and over the bottom strand of the right-hand loop.

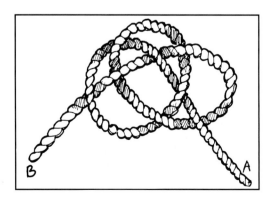

Sequence: Under one, over one, under one, over one.

• How you pull it determines the final form: If you pull up the loop and position the knot at the bottom, it looks like A.

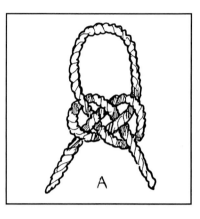

• Tighten the knot to form at the top and it comes out like B.

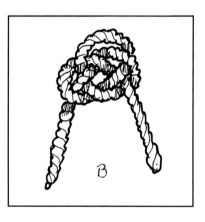

• Or you can tighten the knot around your finger to form a loop to slip over the neck of a tassel (C).

Josephine Knot

This is a carrick bend made with two ends. It's a great tassel knot either used flat on the holding cord or doubled over to form a round head.

- Start by forming a loop with cord A.

- Lay cord B over the loop and under the left end of cord A.

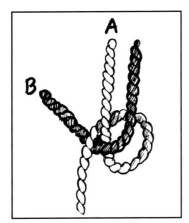

- Cord B then goes back over A, under the top side of loop A, over itself, and under the other side of loop A.

- Another knot can be placed directly below the first one for use on the holding cord.

Sequence: Over one, under one, over one, under one. Once again, how you pull it determines the final form:

- Pull the ends evenly to form a knot on the holding cord.

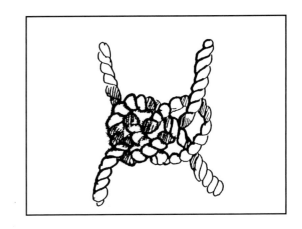

- Pull all the ends to the bottom and wrap to form the head of a tassel.

- Or two knots can be placed side by side by forming knots on each cord.

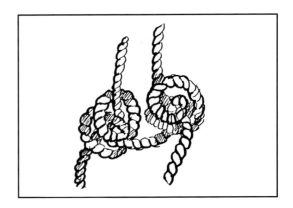

Oriental Mat Knot

Oriental mat knots include a large number of interwoven flat knots sometimes referred to as "pretzel mats." A relatively easy rectangular shape, this one can be used flat on the cord or pulled to form a flat tassel head.

- Fold two cords in half so each forms a loop with the left end over the right end.

Oriental Mat Knot

- Place left loop A over right loop B diagonally.

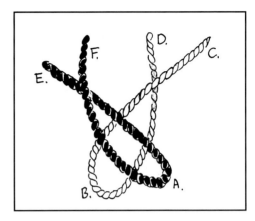

- Put the end of right cord C under end D, over both sides of loop A, and under and through loop B.

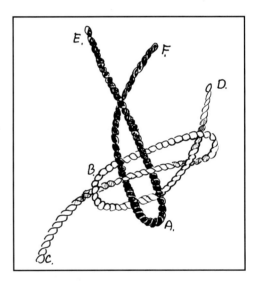

- Pull end E down and over end F, under B, over C, under D, and over loop A.

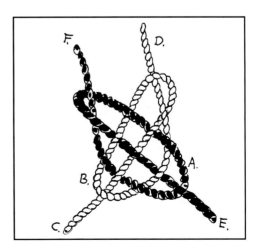

- Work the four ends individually by keeping two ends up and two ends down until the knot is formed on the cord.

Or form it as a tassel top by folding the top ends down.

Any combination of mat or flat knots can be used to form the tops for Oriental-style tassels. They look richer if at least two strands of firm cord are used. In India, mat knots are used as the ends of the tassel.

Dragonfly Knot

Dragonfly-knotted silk tassels decorate the metal hooks that support a bamboo shade. (Japan)

- Form a loop in the center of cord A.

- Fold the lower end over itself, then under loop A to make another loop B.

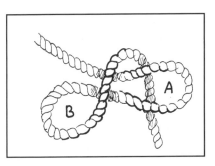

- Form the other end into a loop and pull it through loop A.

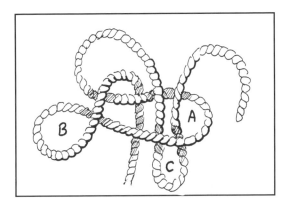

- Keep the working end to the right and up. Weave it over itself and into the loop just formed (C), under the other side of loop C, over the first end and over the right side of loop B, then under the left side of loop B.

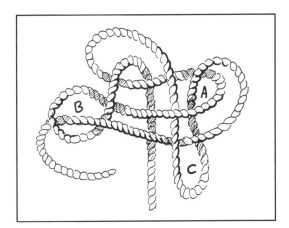

- Continuing with the same end, go under the beginning end, then under, and into loop C.

- Pull the outer loops to form the dragonfly.

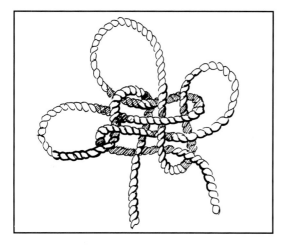

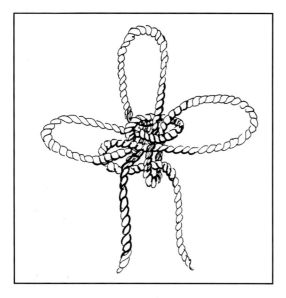

Loose Ends

- All flat mat knots are easier to form if pinned to a board the first go around. Tighten each loop as you work. The excess can be pulled up when you're finished.

- Start with at least a three-foot piece of cord if you intend to do several knots above the tassel. The extra length can be cut off, but adding a cord in the middle of a knot is tricky.

KNOTS WITHOUT WORDS

Either knots are fun or they are knot! Here are a few more for the holding cord.

Knot One

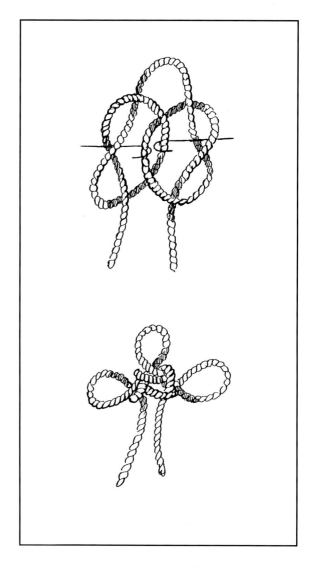

Knot Two

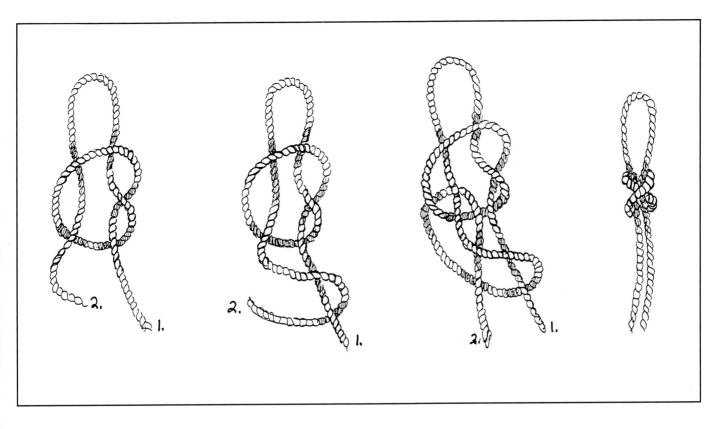

Knot Three

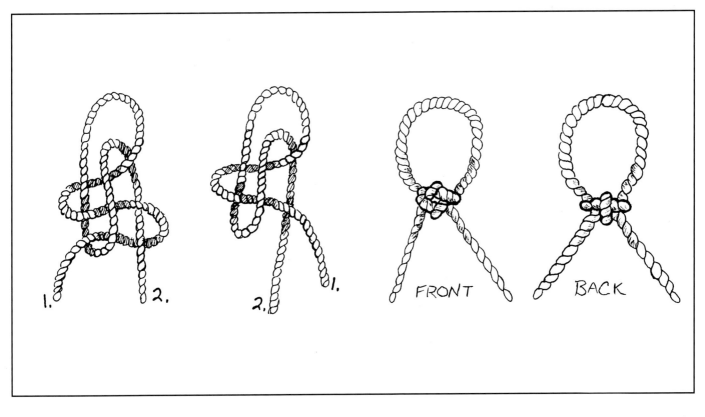

CYLINDRICAL KNOTS

When formed on the holding cord, these are called "stopper" or "lanyard" knots. All knots, but especially stopper knots, look much better tied with crisp yarns; fuzzy ones obliterate the design. Once again, after you tie the knot, try it in various positions.

Overhand "Quipu" or Counting Knot

What could be simpler than an overhand knot? A double overhand knot appears on the end of Korean tassel cords. It is made by tying a regular overhand knot but looping the cord through twice. Hold the very end of the cord with one hand and ease the knot down on itself with the other hand.

Try wrapping it two or more times before tightening and you will have a quipu (kee-poo). The Incas of Peru, who had no written language, used this knot for calculating and recording their accounts. Each wrap represented a unit. Professional quipu keepers aligned the knots on cords to keep records; you can keep a secret accounting on your holding cord. Try it on the end of a thick elegant rope to serve as a tassel.

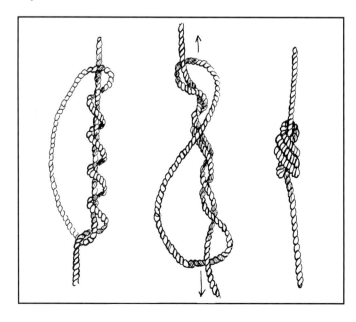

The simple overhand knot was also important to the Arapaho Indians, the Chinese, and the ancient Hebrews. A Huichol Indian legend says that if a woman has had lovers, she must tie knots for each one on a string. She takes this string to a sacred fire and repeats the name of each man recorded. The string is then tossed into the fire, and her sins are forgiven (a handy knot to know).

Three-Strand Wall Knot

This knot can be used as a stopper knot on the cord or placed above or below a mat knot. Use three strands to form it on the holding cord. Using different colors will help you to follow the sequence. To make a wall knot into a tassel head, divide the tassel yarns into thirds and work as if each third were one strand. When the knot is complete, fold the ends down and wrap to form the neck and skirt.

- To start, tie a piece of string on the cord (or clump of yarns) just below where the knot will be. This gives a base against which to work. You can clip off the string if it shows when the knot is completed or use a pretty ribbon and let it become part of the tassel. If the knot is to be the head, gauge the length so when you tie the knot you will still come out even on the skirt ends. If you miss and the top part turns out too short, just make a two-tiered tassel.

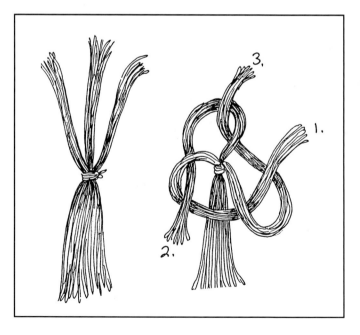

Sequence:

- Strand 3 goes under 2.

- 2 goes around 3 and under 1.

- 1 then goes under and into the loop formed by 3.

- 2 goes under 3 and under and through the loop formed by 1.

- Pull each end evenly until the knot is tight.

Four-Strand Wall Knot

(See notes under Three-Strand Wall Knot.) For a holding cord, fold two strands in half, work the four ends into the knot, and use the loop for the hanger. Add other four-strand knots under the wall knot before you add the tassel. When used as the head, it makes a more complex looking knot when the ends are folded over and the loops are cut to form the skirt.

Sequence:

- 1 goes under 4 and 2.

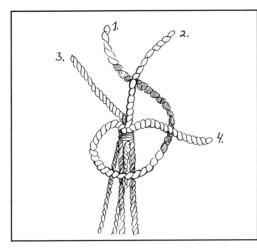

- 2 goes under 1 and 3, and through the loop of 1.

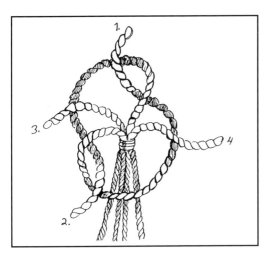

- Next, 3 goes under 1 and 2, through the loop formed by 1, then wraps over 4.

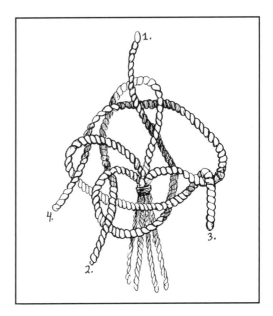

- 4 goes up under 1 and 2, through the loop formed by 2, and under and through the loop formed by 3.

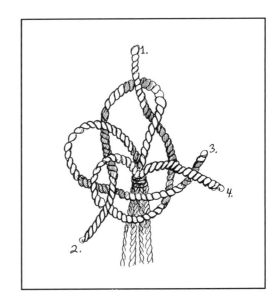

Four-Strand Diamond Knot

This makes a crisp interwoven knot on a two strand (four ends) holding cord. One side is more interesting than the other. To use it as a tassel head, divide the tassel yarns into four sections. Tie the knot, fold the ends down, and use the "square" as the head—either straight

up or bent forward—before wrapping the neck. (Helpful hints: Use two colors to help see the sequence. Tie a string below where the knot will be.)

- Start with an S formation (3 and 4).

- Bend strand 1 over the top of the S and under the bottom loop of the S.

- Bend strand 2 over the bottom leg of the S and under upper loop of the S.

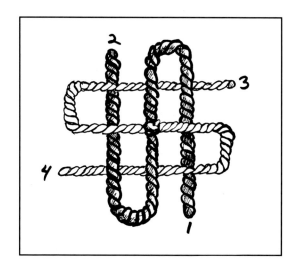

- Then tuck each end clockwise into the adjoining loop by going under and over.

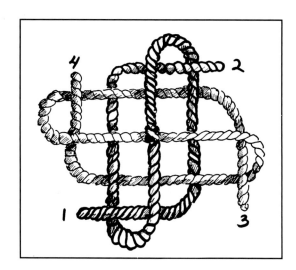

Braided crown knot tassel

- Pull all four ends equally to snug the knot in place and to keep a square look.

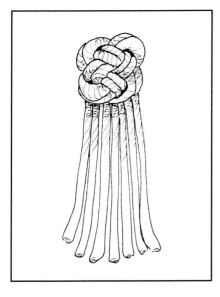

KNOTS FOR TASSEL TOPS

Many knots make interesting tassel heads. Some can be bent to face forward, creating a flat back (handy for attaching to a flat surface—such as a lapel—or just to give a different look).

Overhand Knot

A simple top is made by tying the whole clump of tassel yarns in an overhand knot. Smooth it out, bend it over, and wrap the neck. This knot makes an elegant tassel head. It looks far more complicated than it is. The knot has two sides, so before you bend it, decide which is to be the top. For variety, try making several loops, as in the quipu knot, before folding over and wrapping.

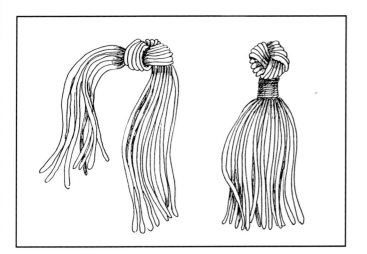

Italian Knotted Tassels

Traditionally tied with fine linen, these delightful little ornamental tassels have been used since the Renaissance on cutwork and lace and are often found on Italian linens and purses.

- Tie overhand knots along a length of linen.

- Then retie over the existing knots.

- Take care to place each knot precisely. Tighten only when it is exactly where you want it.

- Then, tie several lengths together to form tassels.

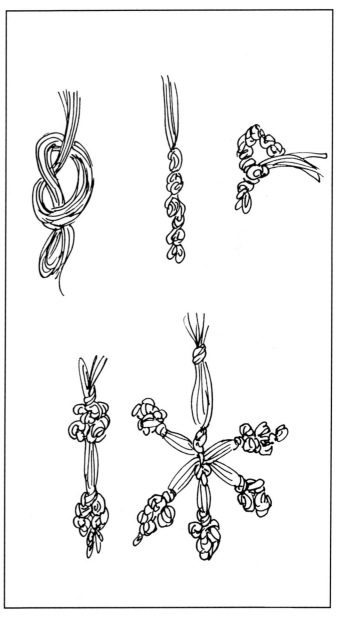

- Sometimes these are suspended from a small buttonhole-covered bead.

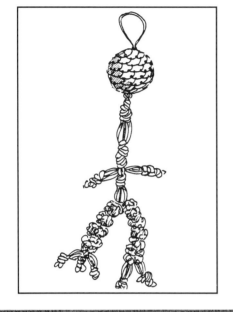

- A variation is the twisted knot tassel also found on Italian linens.

- Make a loop with doubled thread between your thumb and forefinger.

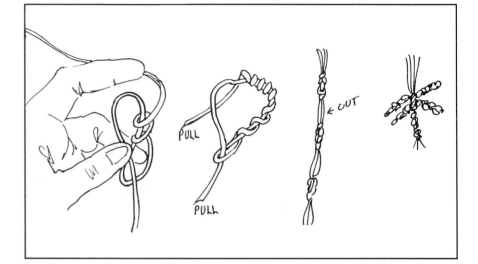

Italian knotted tassels by Vima Micheli

- Bring the working end through the loop seven times.

- Remove it from your finger and pull the ends so that the loop disappears.

- Make another knot close to the first knot. Continue until you have a long string of knots.

- Cut them apart in pairs.

- Start a new string of knots, threading the pairs on as you go. These clusters can be attached to a decorative head or simply left as is. When these knots are tied very close together, they form pompons.

Figure Eight Knot

Almost as easy as an overhand knot, the figure eight knot makes a flatter design. Tie this knot in the center of tassel yarns to form the head. Round it out or use it flat.

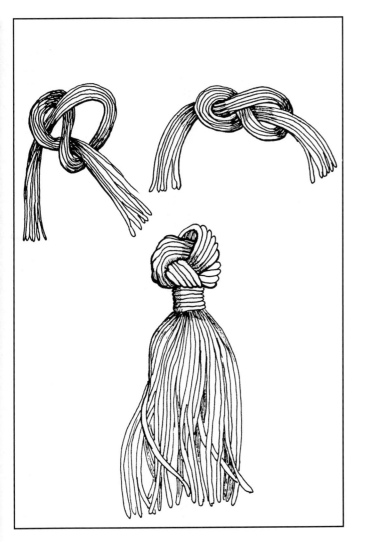

Crown or Friendship Knot

The crown knot is similar to a diamond knot, but the ends will be pointed up. They need to be folded down with the knot at the top, then wrapped to form the tassel head. Bend it forward to make a flat back for pinning to a garment. This is an interesting knot when worked in two colors.

- Wind half the tassel yarns in one color and the other half in another color.

- Lay out all the first color yarns in an N formation and use all the second color yarns to interweave, starting at the bottom right.

- Weave to the left, under and through the loop of the N, then over both strands of the other leg of the N.

- Come back to the right, under all three legs, and turn back to the left, over the first two legs and under the third remaining leg.

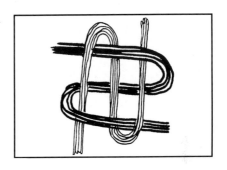

- Pull up evenly on all four strands to center the knot.

Square   *Cross*

Sequence: Under 1, over 2, under all three, over 2, and under 1.

There are two sides ("square" or "cross") to this knot, so choose the one you like best for the top.

Fold the other ends down and wrap under the knot to form a neck or continue in the same manner to form a braid or a longer head for the tassel as in the braided crown knot. This knot is also called a success knot (so don't give up).

Crown knot folded forward

Braided Crown Knot

Crown knots tied one on top of the other make a splendid tassel head. If the knot is tied in one direction continuously, a rounded head develops. If the knot is tied first in a clockwise direction, then in a counterclockwise direction (alternating each time), a square head will develop.

Using two colors and tying all knots either clockwise or counterclockwise creates a round braid with the colors spiraling along the length.

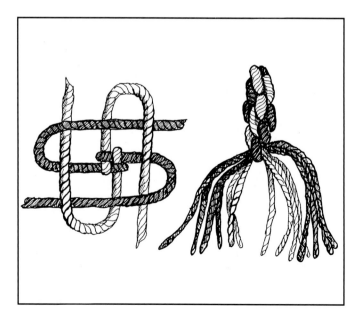

If you alternate the clockwise and counterclockwise knots, one on top of the other, you will make a square braid with vertical stripes.

When alternating the knots, it's easy to forget which one you just tied. Notice the alignment at the center of the knot; the pattern tells you whether you've just made a clockwise or a counterclockwise move.

Sequence: Under 1, over 2 (through the loop), and under 1 (of each leg).

Pull up on all four ends to complete one round. Repeat the knot either in one direction or in an alternating pattern, tightening each time until the braid reaches the desired height for the tassel head. Wrap the neck. This is one tassel you can really grab on to!

Back-Spliced Rope Tassel

This knot is a little tricky but makes a sturdy tassel head or a strong handle.

- Start with a thick three-ply rope. If you have a rope machine, you can make your own.

- Tie off the center of the rope (in the same color as the rope so it won't show).

- Make another tie at the length you want for the head. Try 2" or 3" (5 or 7.5 cm) for a start. All the yarn below this tie will be unraveled to form the tassel.

- Separate the upper section above the center knot into three plies of rope.

- Weave each strand in turn diagonally down through the plies of the rope in an over-one, under-one sequence until you reach the bottom tie.

- When the three sections are woven through the head, wrap all the ends to form a neck.

- Unply the yarns to form the skirt and trim the ends.

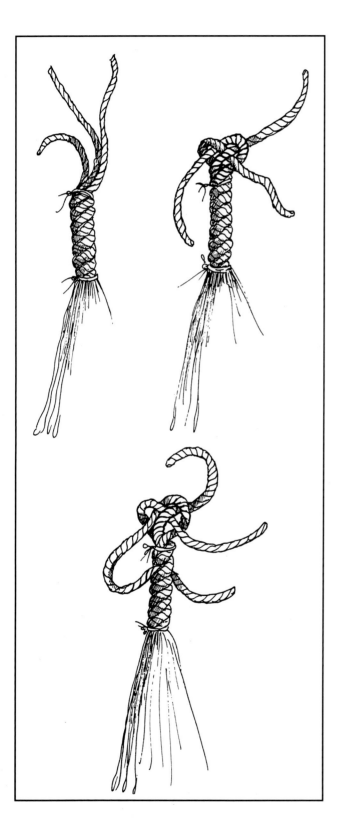

Turk's Head Knot

A widely used knot, the turk's head is basically a woven circle and is quite versatile. You can form it separately and make it into a ring to put around a tassel neck (metallic cord is nice for this). When it's formed on a cord, the turk's head becomes a stopper knot. If it's pulled up tight, it serves as a tassel top. Left flat, it makes a mat knot. How you pull the ends will make the difference. The Chinese button and the monkey fist are turk's head knots pulled to create beads.

- Start the knot at one end of the cord so as to leave a long working end. The starting end will be stationary (SE).

Turk's head knotted tassel heads

• Figure 1 shows the basic pattern. The long end loops around and forms a fourth loop (Fig. 2).

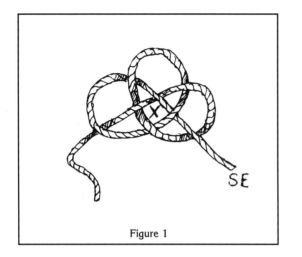

Figure 1

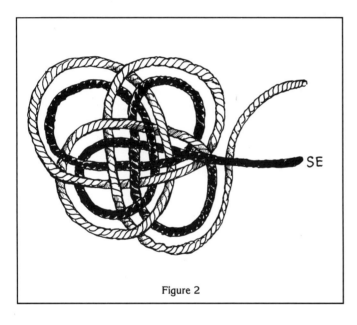

Figure 2

• Weave this end over, under, over, and under, following the basic pattern until the working end reaches the stationary end. Check that every part of the interlocking loops has two rows.

• Repeat the process until the knot is as large as you want. Just be sure that each section has the same number of rows. It is now in the form of a mat.

• Do the final pull up over the finished object (the head or neck of a tassel).

To use the turk's head as a tassel head, stuff the center of the mat with cotton, a bead, or the folded ends

of the tassel top itself. (The folded ends must be securely tied at the fold before pulling them up into the turk's head top.)

To work it as a ring, put your finger, your fist (depending on the size you need), or the neck of a tassel into the center hole (X on Fig. 1). Follow the same set pattern around, working with the long end and keeping the rows even and orderly. Position the ring where it is to remain, then work up tight. If it's very tight, the ends can be cut and they'll be secure, but if it's a loose ring, glue or sew the ends.

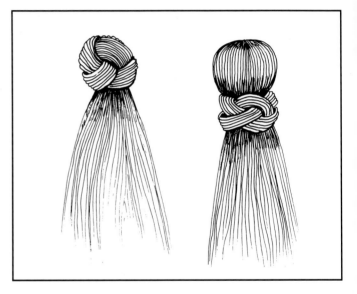

A group of turk's heads can form their own tassel.

The old Afghan tassel hanging (left) has many more tassels than the new (right), and each is topped with several turk's head rings and an integrated knot section. The new hanging has larger, simpler knots and eliminates the turk's head entirely.

Macramé Tops

The Arabs developed macramé, but the sailors of the world perpetuate this handsome craft. The tall ships have all but vanished, yet this precise skill persists. It was popular in the 1970s, so check your library for books on the subject.

Macramé knots can be used as a decorative head, neck, or holding cord for a tassel. Choose smooth, non-fuzzy cords for the knotting. Working cords must be in multiples of four and should be about six times the length of the finished area. Heavy cord and half-hitches will use more material than thinner yarn and square knots. It's better to err by having them too long than too short; extra length can be cut off.

To encase the head and form a holding cord as an integral part of a tassel:

• Wind and cut the yarns for the body of the tassel.

• Place long working cords to knot for the head on top of the tassel yarns.

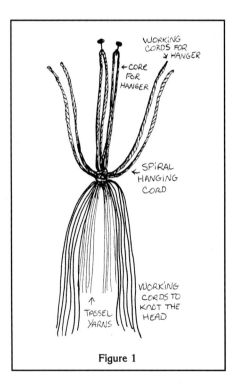

Figure 1

• Add a core the length of the hanger and two or more long cords to work over them to form the hanger.

• Tie the bundle together with an overhand or square knot using the core and hanger cords (Fig. 1).

• Pin the hanger cords securely to a working surface.

• Use the long cords in the tassel bundle to knot a decorative head using any combination of macramé knots.

• End with a row or two of double half-hitches.

• Knot the hanger cords over the core to form a decorative handle (Fig. 2). (Also see the spiral hanging cord illustration.)

Figure 2

Macramé heads also can be made separately over a large bead or a thread spool. When the knotting is complete, remove the form and slip the decorative head over the tassel yarns.

Spiral Hanging Cord

You'll need two sets of cords. The inner ones form a stationary core the length of the finished handle. Pin these firmly to a working surface. The outer cords that form the hanger are the working ends and need to be about six times longer.

To form a spiral to the right:

• The outside left cord A

goes over the core and to the right. Cord B goes over A, then under the core and through the loop formed by cord A.

- Tighten by pulling on both cords.

- Repeat with cord B going across the core and cord A wrapping around cord B, then under the core and through the loop.

- Repeat this sequence, always placing the cord on the right on top (even as it twists) and tightening the knot each time. Continue working to the desired length.

- Clip and glue the ends or fold over and wrap securely.

To spiral the cord in the opposite direction, start with the left outside cord. Even if you choose not to make a macramé head, the spiral cord makes a nice hanger.

A KNOT FOR THE NECK:
Mariner's Whisk Knot

The rate at which a boat moves is measured in "knots" because early mariners tossed a rope overboard that was knotted every 47'3" (14.4 m); after 28 seconds, they counted the knots, thus calculating the ship's speed.

This simple interlacing technique was used to make whisk brooms on sailing ships.

- Divide the tassel or skirt yarns into seven equal parts.

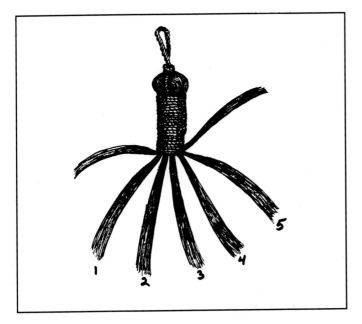

Braided and wrapped sisal tassel used as a whisk broom. Sailors used this construction to form bell pulls and whisks.

- Section 1 goes under 2 and is pulled down.

- Section 2 goes over 1, under 3, and is pulled down.

- Section 3 goes over 2, under 1, and down.

- Continue all the way around.

- The final section goes into the original loop formed by 1 and 2.

- Pull each section to tighten and straighten.

- Securely wrap below the section.

Remember that other knots such as the turk's head also can be used around a tassel's neck.

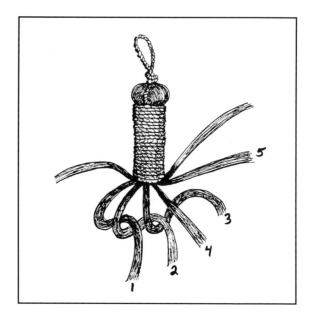

Tassels on the window of a boat

THE GRANNY KNOT

For a "grand" finale on knots and to celebrate my new status in life, here is the "granny" knot...

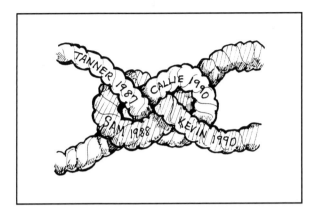

Marilyn Green says, "I have been trying to master this knot since Girl Scout days. Hurrah! Finally made it!"

LOOSE ENDS

- For a more substantial look, double or triple the working strand and work all the strands together as one.

- Work the knot with a single strand. Then—using the same strand—follow the design around completely again and even again.

- Remember to remove all slack from a completed knot to snug it up and produce a firm shape.

Bell-wringer tassel

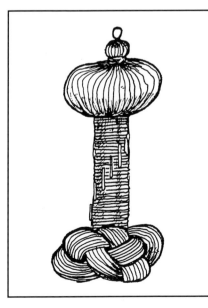

- A Chinese gentleman found a practical use for knotted tassels by wearing them on his belt. The top was a compass followed by an elaborate knot that supported two silk tassels. These tassels contained everything a gentleman might need for a long journey: earpick, chopsticks, scissors, knife, etc. (sort of a tool and toilet-kit tassel).

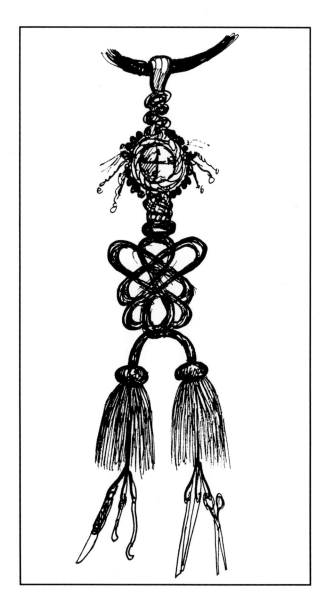

- Like braids, knots can be as frustrating as they are fascinating. While you may need a quiet place, a good reference book, lots of firm cord, and infinite patience to practice, eventually they'll begin to seem like old friends. Knots have been around for a very long time. Ethnologists tell us that even our Paleolithic ancestors mastered a few simple knots.

- When all else fails, improvise. All you'll be doing is inventing a new knot that you can name for yourself, and you don't need to tell anyone how you did it! Knots were often carefully guarded secrets. Ashley says that complicated knots were explained only under pledge of secrecy and that knowledge of one knot was often bartered for that of another.

In Greek legend, Circe gave Ulysses a stout and magic knot. In early Roman times, knots were used as padlocks; when a merchant or nobleman left his building, he would tie his own signature knot to lock the door. When he returned, he would check the knot to see whether anyone had entered during his absence.

REFERENCES

Boy Scout Manuals and books on macramé and sailors' knots cover hundreds of knots. Here are a few I have used:

- *The Ashley Book of Knots*, by Clifford Ashley, Doubleday, 1944.

You might call it "The Bible" of knots; it's very thorough and has good diagrams and written instructions.

- *Encyclopedia of Knots and Fancy Rope Work*, by Graumont and Hensel, Cornell Maritime Press, 1939 and on.

This one has technical pictures of completed work but not much on how to make knots.

- *The Book of Ornamental Knots*, by John Hensel, Scribner, 1973.

Clear pictures, good text. Finished uses for knots including Oriental hangings with tassels.

- *Knots, Useful and Ornamental*, by George Russell Shaw, MacMillan, 1979.

Has good, easy to understand diagrams but has no photos of completed or in-progress work.

Although these books were published awhile ago, knots are knots and they don't change. The library is a resource. Pick a book that makes sense to you and go for it!

Tassel Gallery

O ne of the nice things about tassels is the people who make and collect them. R. H. Brecht at Corona Decor in Seattle says, "Making tassels is fun, especially since you know that so many people receive enjoyment out of using them." Ms. Brecht makes large red and gold tassels for Christmas, designs tassels for theatrical productions, and also supplies Disneyland with tassels. In fact, she sells over one hundred thousand tassels a year, which adds up to a lot of enjoyment.

This chapter will give you a chance to meet other people like Ms. Brecht, who have discovered that tassels can add pleasure to their lives. Many have included their addresses in the back of the book, in case you would like to contact them regarding their work. Respect their art, use it for inspiration, but create only your own unique tassels.

Some of the pieces may seem to stretch the definition of tassel. These have been included to encourage you to reach beyond preconceived ideas and familiar techniques.

Tassels by Rita Zerull

THE MERWITZ FACTORY

Like butterflies emerging from their cocoons, splendorous tassels are metamorphosed in the archaic Merwitz textile factory in Chicago. A glance around the dirt and grime of many years reveals rich, confection-like forms amidst antique equipment. Clanking old metal and wooden looms slowly produce inches of elaborate braid and woven trims.

Sweat shirt clad women are dotted about, meticulously tying silk, wool, rayon, or cotton tassels onto the loom-woven trims. In one corner, two young men stand over a steaming vat of dye, repeatedly dipping large skeins of yarn until the precise shade required by a customer is achieved. Dyed skeins of luscious silk and wool snuggle in one area, while in another ten different textures of rayon await their turn in the dye bath.

Meanwhile, two men in the basement string miles of yarns onto a rope machine. Each strand is counted and precisely placed. Recipe cards for thirty styles of rope hang on the wall, specifying the number of twists for the filler, the number of ends for covering yarns, and the turns of the rope wheel for each yard of completed cord. This is an exact process. Each group of fibers on the wheel is tied at two-foot intervals along the entire length of each ply. The rope machine is turned two or three times, then the ties are removed, retied, and turned again until all twenty-seven yards of cord are completed.

Following the birth of a tassel—from job order, through custom dyeing, wrapping of molds, twisting of bullion fringe, and tying of the tassel, to final assembly of all these elements into a gorgeous object—is a fascinating experience. On the day I visited Merwitz, the people there were working on an order for Henri Bendel; the tiebacks for that order, needless to say, were costly.

Who can afford this painstakingly crafted material? Well, millionaire publisher Hugh Hefner once placed an order with Merwitz to decorate his airplane.

An assortment of tassels from Merwitz

Each tiny tassel is tied off by hand at Merwitz

Preparing the rope machine to produce luscious tassel cords

CAROLYN SCHULTZ

Fashioning wheat and straw into tassels is an old folk craft, one which is still practiced in major grain-growing areas of the world. These tassels symbolize the spirit of the harvest and the fertility of the earth.

Economical, country-crafted items of this type (known as "corn dollies" in England) offer new ideas for using old techniques to make tassels. Carolyn Schultz became interested in wheat weaving while she was in Oxford, England.

After settling in Kansas, she became even more involved with the craft during a centennial commemo-

rating the arrival of Russian Mennonites. These people immigrated in 1874, seeking religious freedom and bringing with them the hard, winter wheat (Turkey Red) that helped make Kansas the breadbasket of the world. Harvest tassels, fashioned from this wheat, were a part of the 1974 centennial celebration.

As a result, Carolyn wrote *Wheat Weaving Made Easy* and now operates the campus granary of the Mennonite's Bethel College Women's Association, which provides wheat as well as instructions for carrying on this tradition in America.

Opposite page: A lantern-style tassel found in England, Guatemala, Mexico, and Greece

Left: The Indians of South America use this style ("Corazon de Trigo" or "heart of wheat") in their places of worship.

Below: British farmers plaited harvest knots or buttonhole favors for their sweethearts. In some areas, the fertility tradition is still maintained; while knots made for women include the grain, only straw is used in knots made for men.

DAVID AND BOBBE MCCLURE

We've all heard of the Stone Age and the Iron Age, but what about the Age of Fiber? Long before man learned to use bronze, he harvested vines and grasses to make snares and nets, to lash shelters, and to hold skins about his body. Along with leather, hair, and bark, these fibers were some of man's first tools.

David and Bobbe McClure are contemporary artists who bring us up-to-date on the use of grasses. Nature may be the original tassel maker, but these two artists have certainly enhanced the plain old cornstalk. By adding handsome cedar tops to the natural tassels of the broomcorn plant, an entirely new tassel is formed. Because the McClures use durable natural fibers such as tampico cactus, sotol lily, and rice roots to create these wonderful forms, the finished pieces function as ornate but utilitarian brooms and brushes. Their simple, elegant designs are an inspiration for all tassel makers.

Exquisite brushes by David and Bobbe McClure

CINDY SPOLEK AND GREG WELLS

I am delighted to share the work of Cindy Spolek and Greg Wells—two creative Santa Fe designers who hold a very special place in my heart. They are members of Aid to Artisans, a group dedicated to providing a market outlet for native crafts; its profits go directly to the artisans.

"We travel a lot, and ethnic cultures are our favorite sources of inspiration," Cindy says. "Beads from India, African mudcloth, Guatemalan textiles, Native American beadwork, eastern European embroideries, and tassels from everywhere are materials we love and collect to use in our clothing. The hand-crafted works of tribal peoples are not reproducible by modern techniques. It is the labor-of-love handwork, combined with native motifs and color sense, that keep our creative fires kindled."

Cindy designs lush shearling coats, jackets, and vests, while Greg creates incomparable shearling boots and shoes. Tassels adorn these stunning garments. For the most part, these two artists use ethnic tassels, but they also make some themselves from rolled and fringed suede with beads added.

Cindy designs her shearling coats to include tassels; tassels embellish Greg's shearling boots.

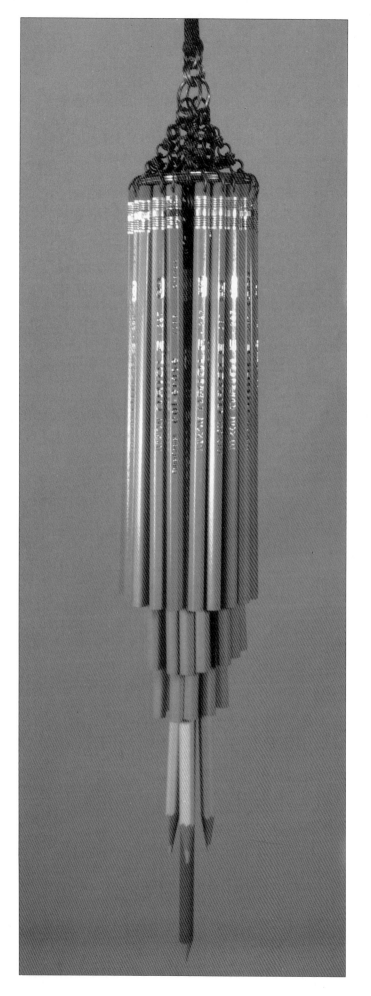

DAVID LAPLANTZ

It's difficult to imagine tassels being controversial, but in the hands of jewelry artist David LaPlantz, anything can happen. David describes himself as the product of a World War II romance between Bernice and Milton LaPlantz:

"My fondest memories are of riding my bicycle through alleys, checking out garbage barrels for finds. Going to the dump with my dad on Saturday mornings was the highlight of the week."

David's specialty is jewelry made from anodized aluminum and chain mail. So what should we expect when he turns his artistic talents to tassels?

"Remember those large pencils we had in first grade? They seemed so big—like holding a telephone pole—just to put some scratches on large lined paper. And now today I am here in front of a computer keyboard tapping a bunch of small keys to write this account of my tassels. How far we have come in such a short time.

"In making this tassel, I have gathered together all of those memories along with some neat pencils and iron chain mail to create a shimmering visual treatment of the common (or not so common) pencil. The simplicity of the pencil is still magic to me. May we never lose that special magic implied in the simple objects of life." Like pencils and tassels!

Pencil tassel

JOHN SKARE

No one knows better than weaver John Skare that tassels are the natural conclusion of wrapped warp-ends. Rather than cut off and seam the edges of his colorful jackets, John leaves his warp fringes to provide a decorative and textural finish. The warps are wrapped at one-inch intervals along the ends, leaving short tassels. To produce longer tassels on the selvedge, John extends the wefts beyond the edges as he weaves, then wraps and shapes them. He saves all his thrums and uses them to provide additional tassels to hold the garment panels together.

John has won several awards from the Handweavers Guild of America as well as a gold medal for weaving from the Norwegian American Museum. He is a full-time professional weaver who works under the trade name "Clothman." This name evolved when he was introduced to a group of pastors as a man showing his cloth to men of the cloth. Now he makes cloth for human forms, interior walls, floors, and furnishings. His work is characterized by a subtly blended color palette and (of course) those wonderful textural tassels.

"Whenever I'm asked to comment on the nature and significance of my work, I begin to feel a little uneasy," said John. "Maybe it is because I feel more comfortable with yarn and looms than I do with words. Perhaps my work can speak for itself. People who try my coats on say, 'I feel like dancing,' or 'I want to extend my arms and fly.' Most wearables artists feel that people animate their work, but I feel that it is my work that is animating the people. I'd like to think it's magic."

Bottom left: **Old Rose Greatcoat**

Bottom right: **Cardinal**

Below: **Wiger Coat**

HOULÈS

Houlès et Cie is a fine French designer and manufacturer of tassels for home decoration. The Houlès's interest in textiles may have begun as early as 1650, when John-Baptiste Houlès was introduced to Master Poquelin, King Louis XIV's first tapestry maker. By the end of the last century, the Houlès family had established a shop in Paris that served as a creative center for interior designers.

Today, Susanne Houlès is the force behind the company, which creates tassels and trimmings that are distributed worldwide. She says, "Within the tradition of French design, tassels play a significant role. Today there is a growing desire for the warmth, beauty, and individuality in home decoration that trimmings can provide."

Mrs. Houlès designs from a palette of over two thousand colors of yarn. Most of these yarns are cotton combined with viscose to maintain the brightness of color. Beige, she says, is the most popular color, but for the 1990s she has introduced a dramatic black-and-gold metallic line. Much of her inspiration comes from extensive travels and antique sketches and samples.

Left: Layout for a custom interior coordinates fabric with tassel and trimming.

Right: This tieback from the Houlès archives, entitled **Grand Russia,** *was made by nineteenth-century craftsmen from the courts of central Europe.*

SCALAMANDRÉ

The first family of tassels works not in the White House but in a red-brick factory on Long Island, New York. Here, three generations of the Scalamandré family continue in the Italian Renaissance tradition to produce the finest fabrics and trims.

The company was started in 1929 by Franco Scalamandré, who emigrated from Italy in 1927. The first textile he produced in this country was for William Randolph Hearst's San Simeon mansion in California. Scalamandré has been giving advice on and making the finest restorations ever since. Today his daughter Adriana Bitter, her husband, and their four children run the company. The patter of tiny feet can sometimes be heard above the clatter of ancient looms; Scalamandré's fourth generation will continue the family tradition well into the future.

Time is not of the essence at Scalamandré. Here, a single tieback tassel can take two weeks to make. Cords are meticulously twisted and plied by expert craftsmen.

An experienced weaver may spend an hour to produce an inch of complicated tieback and a full day to make four yards of braid.

The price for this excellence and refinement is dear, but as Adriana says, "We make special products. The Scalamandré family is keeping alive old traditions, not just for sentimental reasons, but because there is a real need for quality and elegance in contemporary life. We train our own people so we can create special products, be they custom designed or reproductions of textiles to brighten historic American homes."

And of course, the first family of tassels has been brightening the home of America's first family since the administration of President Herbert Hoover.

Well-known for its museum-quality reproductions, Scalamandré combines impeccable craftsmanship and the finest materials to create some of the world's most elegant tassels.

Ellen Holt's tassels are intricately designed, carefully executed, and luxuriously decorative.

ELLEN S. HOLT

Ellen Holt didn't start out to become one of America's foremost tassel makers. She started as a technical illustrator, then discovered weaving in 1970. She decided to produce high-grade, hand-loomed fabrics for the interior design trade, but the god of tassels intervened. After weaving yardage for a show, Ellen used the leftover warp to make fringe and tassels, and a new career was launched.

"I was reluctant to make them, as they are so labor intensive," she says. "But requests became more and more frequent. The challenges began to present themselves. I found I was not restrained at all in the creative process and could design as I wished."

Ellen and her associates produce a full line of passementeries and have made numerous replications of historical tassels, including those at the Abraham Lincoln home in Springfield, Illinois, and the William Howard Taft home in Cincinnati, Ohio.

"Tassels should not dominate the fabrics for which they are designed, but complement them," says Ellen. "When designing passementeries for highly decorative fabrics, I first view the fabric from at least twenty feet away. This enables me to accomplish four tasks: to determine the scale of the pattern, to study the composition, to define what dominates the viewer's attention, and most importantly, to read the colors and determine the intensity and value of each."

Once she's assembled all this information, she's prepared to create a tassel with "integrity." Her tassels certainly demonstrate the care and work that have gone into making them.

BLACK SHEEP WEAVING SHOP

The Black Sheep shop in Encinitas, California, is a tassel lover's delight. Here among the fabulous yarns and beads you will find at least two tassel artists.

Barbara Chapman is probably responsible for turning most of southern California on to tassels. She's been teaching at Black Sheep for years. Her tassels reflect an ethnic interest expressed through unique embellishment—the wilder and crazier the better. She often incorporates purchased tassels into her own creations. Barbara has a treasure house of wonderful things from all over the world that she also adds to them. Twice a year,

Barbara Chapman combines her own colorful tassels with finds from bazaars around the world.

Top and bottom: Rita Zerull's love of tassels and needle lace is evident in these accessories.

the Chapmans host an open house at which their exceptional creations can be viewed. On these occasions, even the coffee urn is decked out with tassels.

Rita Zerull also teaches at Black Sheep. Her approach is more romantic. One of her passions is needle lace; another is tassels. She artfully combines her two loves to produce exquisite accessories. It all got started, she says, when her children were small:

"I embroidered everything in the house. Then I realized I didn't have to be practical. I saw this incredible tassel—a bright crazy thing—and I just started making them. I ended up putting tassels on everything and giving many away as presents. I must have done thousands, always trying new ideas and techniques. Now—years later—I find the tassel gifts still hanging about friends' and relatives' homes. It is unfathomable but fabulous. They just really do turn people on."

As you can see from Tom Henderson's photographs, Rita's and Barbara's tassels are indeed a turn-on.

An exuberant and imaginative creation by Barbara Chapman (detail at left)

GERDA RASMUSSEN

Gerda Rasmussen makes me believe in fairy god-mothers. One day she waved her tasseled wand and summoned me to her magical studio, a land filled with yarn, fabric, beads, books, and drawers and drawers of mystic treasure.

One of the delights of her studio is to lie on the couch and gaze up at the brilliant canopy of floating tassels. I felt like Cinderella. In the midst of all this blaze of color, good little yarns become grand and gorgeous tassels. And here they live happily ever after, hanging everywhere in this tasseled kingdom.

Gerda was born in Denmark. She came to this country in 1956 and pursued a career in sculpture. In 1975 she was diagnosed as having lead poisoning.

"I felt like my life was over," she said. "But God doesn't close a door without opening another one. Then I saw this book where you take a piece of cardboard and wrap some yarn around and you have a tassel. I went completely wild!" Most of her work is still three-dimensional. Because you can peek in and around her creations, each becomes a visual playground.

Gerda now travels a great deal. She has taught on the cruise ship *Love Boat* and makes frequent trips to Scandinavia. "When I'm traveling, people sit down and do tassels with me. Some people would find this irritating, to always have folks looking you over. But I want to share tasseling with the world because it makes people happy."

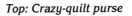

Top: Crazy-quilt purse

Bottom left: No bed would be complete without its fanciful tassels.

Bottom right: Gerda Rasmussen cheerfully surrounds herself with tasseled objects.

Left: Douglas A. MacChestney (Deputy Chief, Highland Games) clad in formal attire. His evening sporran is seal skin and has a seal-skin tassel as well.

Right: The dress sporran is usually made of fur and includes silver ornamentation. The tassel is a silver chain and ball with a fringe of fur to match the sporran.

DOUGLAS A. MACCHESTNEY

We are all aware of the Scottish love of tassels and perhaps curious about the kilt and sporran tassels, so I thought it would be interesting to find out what I could about this unique attire. I couldn't have picked a better source than Douglas A. MacChestney, who has made sporrans for the Lord Provost of Glasgow, the founder of the Shakey's Pizza restaurant chain, and the world champion Scottish fiddler.

Since the kilt has no pockets, the sporran serves as both purse and decoration. According to Doug, most commercial sporrans were not constructed to hold more than a wallet, so he designed and made for himself several that would hold all his "worldly possessions." Before he knew it, he was sending his sporrans all over the United States and the United Kingdom.

There are three basic types of sporrans: everyday, evening or dress, and band or military. Day sporrans and tassels are made of leather or fur, such as muskrat or badger.

HOPE AND PHILIP HOLTZMAN

The expressive tapestry-woven figures by Hope and Philip Holtzman take tassels a step beyond the normal scope and open yet another area for exploration.

"The people who buy our work are very open-minded, very emotional," says Philip. "They are ready to be touched—to be moved. We always have our eyes open for unusual old things to incorporate in our figures."

Hope weaves the intricate tapestries using hand-spun, naturally dyed wool and silk found during the Holtzmans' travels. Philip carves the wooden parts, frequently using old wood. They've been working together for over ten years and produce about twenty figures a year.

"They don't come easily. We do lots of drawings, a lot of little beginnings," Hope adds. "A tassel can bring attention to an area, or it can be a way to finish hanging warps. They need to be used carefully, not arbitrarily. The challenge is to transform the object so that it functions in the piece, rather than calling attention to what it was. We

do whatever is necessary to bring the figure to life. They call on people's attention, but only if they are interested. And attention is like life: it gives something back to you. Like in any ritual, inanimate objects can read back to a person what is necessary."

Her words apply to tassels as well.

Tapestry-woven and carved figures by Hope and Philip Holtzman.

JEFFREY AND KATRINA SEATON

Jeffrey and Katrina Seaton work primarily in rare and exotic woods. These photos—from their tribal series—reflect "inspirations from primitive totemic anthropomorphic images." The tassels, which set these elegant sculptures apart from others, are made from hand-dyed and shredded raffia.

Left: Winter

Bottom left: Lakewood Vigas

Bottom right: Black Vigas

JOAN SCHULZE

Joan Schulze does more than any other artist, homemaker, wife, mother of four, and gardener that I know. She is simply phenomenal. Her exquisite art quilts are exhibited all over the world, and while they go in one direction, Joan seems to be off in another, sharing her considerable teaching talents. You may find it interesting to see the manner in which her busy, creative mind works:

"Tassels have always conjured up opportunities to combine fabric and threads in a whimsical way. I started by choosing fabric, cutting it into strands, layering pieces together, and coming up with fat, luscious color groupings, but they just sat around for weeks in this unfinished state.

"Working on a collage, I needed some of the tassel parts, so I pirated the bottom, leaving just the strands.

"On another day, I was back into the tassel idea. The remnants weren't exciting enough. I picked at them, trying to get an idea. The thought of making the tassels in book form was intriguing. I made two of them and felt like I was on a new track.

"While driving one day, I kept turning the tassels over in my mind. I remember rounding a corner and suddenly recalling an installation of burial poles done by Australian aborigines that I had seen in the National Gallery in Canberra. I knew then exactly how I was going to proceed when I got back home.

"My finished tassel forest became a journal of my Australian memories done in miniature. These tassels can be a metaphor for the experience of traveling down under."

Tassel Forest

Below: Three tassels (from left to right): **Tribal Dancer, Verdegris, Gone Fishing**

Top right: Collage of materials for **Verdegris**

Bottom right: Collage of materials for **Tribal Dancer**

JUDY CONTENT

Judy Content must have come to earth on a rainbow. Everywhere she goes and everything she touches is transformed into a kaleidoscope of color. Whether she's working with her exquisite dyed-silk clothing, making architectural hangings, or borrowing her daughter's crayons to make stunning wall fans, the vibrant color that this tiny, red-haired, blue-eyed elf leaves in her wake truly brightens the world.

Her work is shown internationally and graces many a corporate office and hotel lobby. Judy made the tassels shown here from her hand-painted paper, meticulously rolled and glued to form beads, which she then strung on exotic yarns. They make a delightful melodic sound as they sway in the breeze of her home.

GAIL AND TONY ROSSI

Gail and Tony Rossi spent nine years in China. Gail, a textile artist, researched the folk art of China's Guizhou Province. In order to document folk arts and customs, she explored remote mountainous areas which were inhabited by various minority groups. "Tassels of all sizes and shapes," she notes, "are commonly integrated into traditional costumes and baby carriers in this region." Gail has written a book about the Dong people and was curator for an exhibit of Guizhou minority textiles. She and Tony have organized a foundation to help market and preserve China's unique folk-art traditions and to assist rural education among China's ethnic minorities. The Rossis also lead textile tours to China.

Tassels from Guizhou province (China)

KIM HEE-JIN

Kim Hee-Jin is president of the Korean Maedup (knot) Research Society. In 1976 the government of the Republic of Korea designated her as "Intangible Cultural Property Number Twenty-Two" for her skill in reviving the art of cord and knot making, which is an integral part of Korean tassels. Kim Hee-Jin follows the ancient traditional methods including spinning, dyeing, and braiding the silk cords by hand. To form a cord, she may use up to 1,440 separate threads and may incorporate some thirty-three different knots. It took Mrs. Kim thirteen years of sore and bleeding fingers to master the skills necessary to create these intricate forms. She says, "It has been a lifetime effort and now I have very strong finger muscles." Her work has been shown in Paris, Washington, D.C., Tokyo, and other major cities.

Colorful Korean tassels evolved in the royal court during the "Three Kingdoms" period (57 B.C. to A.D. 668). Royal and noble women wore as many as three brilliant pendant tassels to enliven their clothing. Traditional Korean costumes have no pockets, so everyone—men, women, and children—carried decorative bags with tassel closures, a practice which has continued well into the twentieth century.

She explains that the military used tassels on swords and pendants, while officials often wore chest-high belts with tassels that reached to the knees. Tassels were used in the home as tiebacks on mosquito nets, as decorations on fans and musical instruments, and on elaborately knotted wall hangings. They were hung on court palanquins as well as ordinary carriages, and they still appear today on funeral hearses.

Korean tassels have lovely names, such as "strawberry" (used on men's belts), "button," "phoenix," "bee," and even "octopus" tassel.

In lieu of pockets, Koreans used purses. The lavender one is for a man, and the green-red gold foil one is for a woman.

KENNETH KING

I could easily bestow the title "King of Tassels" on Kenneth King. His customers—among them Elton John, Rob Lowe, and Cloris Leachman—would no doubt agree, for this man is a master of meticulous detail.

Kenneth started his fashion career designing sculptural hats, but he has since branched out into clothing and accessories. To highlight his pieces he adds exquisitely detailed tassels. Currently he is adding tassels to his home furnishings which—like everything else he painstakingly crafts—are fit for a king. He uses tassels for a variety of reasons but says his two main ones are:

"...The movement they provide. My pieces, because of the engineering, are somewhat rigid. The movement of a tassel can echo the movement of the lines of a design, as well as provide some fluid movement as a counterpoint to the structural rigidity of the piece."

"...The weight they give. This is from either a visual or engineering standpoint. Visually, they provide a strong, vertical grounding point at the base of a composition. From an engineering standpoint, they can control the hang or drape of a piece."

Top: A stunning tasseled footstool

Bottom right and left: Superb tassels echo movement in Kenneth King's designs. Photographer: John Bagley Model: Loretta Simmons

EDWARD DYAS

The story read, "Dyas does all the work himself—right down to the tassels—all five thousand of them." Now that was someone I wanted to know! So I started a correspondence with award-winning costume designer Edward Dyas of Melbourne, Australia. As it turned out, there were "only" five hundred tassels on this one piece; Edward apologized and sent me a picture anyway. He hopes to come to the United States and design for the movies. Melbourne has only one costume ball a year, so he has little chance to show off his flamboyant pieces there.

Edward says, "I am greatly influenced by the work of Erté and most recently by the illustrations of Antonio Lopez. I use any unusual material to give the desired look and make most items. Rarely must I buy them. I design only within my production capabilities."

When he's not snipping tassels, he's clipping articles about film stars for his international clients who collect such stories and pictures.

Above: Griffin costume with over five hundred handmade tassels of various sizes (view from rear)

Right: Tasseled creations by Edward Dyas

Opposite page: Mardi Gras mask emphasizes jeweled tassels

feels that the acid from wooden molds is detrimental to fiber and would like to see ceramic or some other inert material substituted.

"Tassels are an art form," he says, "and as such should be signed by the maker. This will make museums take notice and document their history. How many unsigned paintings are hung in museums and galleries? An artist must sign his work or be forgotten." To this end, Jim has designed a small name tape to attach inside the tassel skirt or on its mold, so that all tassels can be signed by their creators. "A tiny and silly form of immortality perhaps, but without it, how can artistic credit be given accurately?" Something to remember as you make your next tassel.

Top portion of the archival tag that Jim Rankin attaches to each tassel in his collection.

ARCHIVAL PROVENANCE TAG

DO NOT REMOVE THIS TAG
IT IS AN HISTORICAL RECORD FOR
PRESENT AND FUTURE OWNERS.

IDENTITY AND HISTORY: This tassel was one of a group which adorned the face of the Teaser curtain in a movie palace in Milwaukee: The WARNER Thea. in 1931 when it opened. The theatre was renamed the CENTRE Thea. in 1966 and was divided into two theatres (the CENTRE I&II) in 1973 at which time this tassel and the others which were connected to it, were removed and stored in the theatre until 1989. The theatres were again renamed in 1982 when they became the GRAND CINE-MAS I&II. The drapery contractor in 1931 was the Charles H. Kenney Co. of New York City, but drapers rarely made tassels or other "trimmings"; it is likely that they subcontracted a "Passementier" or Trimmings maker for this skilled craft. To put the value of this unusual art form in perspective, it would cost approx. $350 to have this unique tassel made today. CARE: This and many other forms of passementerie cannot always be cleaned successfully without risk. Gentle vacuuming may be done, but never laundering or water washing. Dry cleaning by a specialist in silks by hand cleaning is possible, but risky! There are sometimes glues used in such tassels which may be softened and released by dry cleaning as well as water. If cleaning is absolutely necessary it should be referred to a professional Textile Conservator. The Museum of Textiles in Wash.D.C., or the Curator of Textiles at a local museum can recommend a Conservator. Never display this tassel in sunlight or near hot lights or heat vents or drafts. Never store it in a basement or attic, nor sealed in plastic where moisture and mildew might occur; but a plastic covering which has holes at top and bottom to promote air circ. would serve to reduce dust and grime. The suspending cord is secured to the wooden core, or "mold" as it is called

JAMES H. RANKIN

If there's such a thing as an environmentalist, conservationist, and "Ralph Nader" of tassels, then Jim Rankin is our man. As historian and advocate, he has embarked upon a one-person crusade to rescue the unacknowledged, maligned tassel.

"It all started in a Milwaukee movie palace (those luxurious theaters of the Roaring Twenties)," he begins. "I saw my first tassels and became fascinated with their unique opulence in the blend of the sensuous curves of the body coupled with the lush ebullience of the skirt of bullion-style fringe." (Now, those are the words of a true tassel lover!)

To preserve the history and provide proper care for each tassel in his collection, Jim attaches an archival tag that describes the tassel and how best to preserve it. He

On The Fringe

Fiber is a truly universal language. I've sat in many plazas and airports—holding only a piece of yarn—and have instantly made wordless contact with other people. A tassel can be quickly constructed and given as a gesture of international friendship. Learning the various words for tassel, however, may prove somewhat of a challenge. These translations have been given to me by the people of the world; I only hope we were all talking about the same thing. Give them a try and be prepared for a few laughs.

Thailand...pon raya
Holland ....kwast
San Salvador ....trenza
Japan...fusa
Eastern Tibet ....zalo
Germany...................................quaste, troddel
Spain ....borla
Iran ....band
China ....sua
Egypt. ....sharabia
Italy...fiocco
France..gland
Korea ....sul
Tonga. ....kafa
Nepal (hair tassel)..................................dhago
and in Latin...................stalagmium fibriatum

Formal tassels make up these elegant fringes.

Resources

The creative people who have added so much to this book have graciously given their addresses so that you may contact them regarding their work. Many teach workshops or have books and supplies available. Please send a self-addressed, stamped envelope if you wish a reply.

Aardvark
P.O. Box 2449
Livermore, CA 94550
Mail order supplies and books;
"Varkies" shop here

Antique Purse Collectors
Box 572
Campbell, CA 95009
If purses are your bag, this is a neat
group.

Apple Tree Lane
801 La Honda Rd.
Woodside, CA 94062
Tassel-making kits

Aramco Magazine
9009 West Loop South
Houston, TX 77096
Middle Eastern art and affairs

Bahamas Tourist Office
3450 Wilshire Blvd., Suite 208
Los Angeles, CA 90010
Tassels on these tropical islands show
up whenever you run into a policeman
or a festival.

Clotilde Barrett
4475 Laguna Pl. #304
Boulder, CO 80303
Fiber teacher; author

Black Sheep Weaving Shop
1010 1 St.
Encinitas, CA 92024
Worth a visit, it's south of Los Angeles
and north of San Diego.

Virginia L. Blakelock
16510 S.W. Edminston Rd.
Wilsonville, OR 97070
Beading teacher; author; mail order
supplies and beads

Sue Bonnin
2467 W. Lansing Way
Fresno, CA 93705
Beaded tassel kits

British Tourist Authority
350 So. Figueroa St., Suite 450
Los Angeles, CA 90071
Catch a glimpse of royalty in tasseled
livery, watch the changing of the
guard at Whitehall every day at 11
a.m., and study the uniforms of the
Tower of London wardens, which date
from 1552.

Gayle Bryan
643 Foster Ct. #2
Hayward, CA 94544
Quilter

Adele Cahlander
3522 Knox Ave. North
Minneapolis, MN 55412
Author, Sling Braiding of the Andes

Barbara Chapman
c/o Black Sheep Weaving Shop
1010 1 Street
Encinitas, CA 92024

Judy Content
827 Matadero Rd.
Palo Alto, CA 94306
Textile artist; commissions

Liz Turner Deal
2252 W. 29th Ave.
Eugene, OR 97405
Needlework designs and books; mail
order

Helen Dietz
16061 Selborne
San Leandro, CA 94578
Jewelry workshops

D'Kei, Inc.
P.O. Box 446
Lisle, IL 60532
Ready-made tassels and cords; catalog
available

Sara Drower
127 Laurel
Wilmette, IL 60091
Soft-sculpture artist

Edward Dyas
7 Decarle St.
Brunswick, Victoria 3056
Australia
Costume designer; movie buff

Jane Felder
2555 West Bluff Ave.
#138 Lakeview
Fresno, CA 93711
Fiber artist

Gordon Frost
P.O. Box 2
Benicia, CA 94510
Want to know about the textiles and
tassels of Guatemala? Gordon has been
collecting, photographing, and leading
trips to remote villages for years.

Jean Goldberg
5 Kemsley Ct.
Hawthorne East 3123
Victoria, Australia
Fiber artist

Denise Hanlon
4901 Pleasant Valley Rd.
Oakdale, CA 95677
Fiber artist

Charles Hanson, Jr.
Museum of the Fur Trade
HC 74, Box 18
Chadron, NE 69337

Harrower House
P.O. Box 274
Hope, NJ 07844
Ornamental paper trims (gold paper tassels etc.); catalog available

Tom Henderson Photography Studio
11722 Sorrento Valley Rd., Suite A
San Diego, CA 92121

Joy May Hilden
29 Avenida Dr.
Berkeley, CA 94708
Bedouin weaving research

Ruthmarie Hofmann
4448 Winners Circle
Rocklin, CA 95677
Fiber artist

Hope and Philip Holtzman
10 Floribel Ave.
San Anselmo, CA 94960
Commission sculpture

Beth Karjala
1408 North Elizabeth Ave.
Muncie, IN 47304
Author of a book on belts; workshops

Dinah Kelly
12 Park St.
Brighton, BN2 2BS
England
Furniture and carved wood; tassels to order

Christine Kimball
15714 East Fourth Ave.
Veradale, WA 99037
Painter; maker of beaded tassels

Kenneth D. King
1156 Howard St.
San Francisco, CA 94103
Elegant clothing, costumes, and accessories

Candace Kling
127 Monte Cresta Ave.
Oakland, CA 94611
Artist (ribbons and roses a specialty)

Jerry Kreinik
P.O. Box 1966
Parkersburg, WV 26102
Gold threads; mail order

Carol Krieger
466 Braemar Ranch Ln.
Santa Barbara, CA 93109
Doll maker

Pennye Kurtela
653 West Stuart
Fresno, CA 93704
Fiber artist

Laotian Handcraft Center
1579 Solano Ave.
Berkeley, CA 94707
Tassels and wonderful handcrafted items of Mien hill tribes

David LaPlantz
899 Bayside Cutoff
Bayside, CA 95524
Jeweler; author

Lise Lawrence
1128 W. Pierce
Houston, TX 77019
Doll maker

Judy Lehman
Rt. 2, Box 357
Waller, TX 77484
Tassel and needlework teacher

June Linsley
7 High Ridge Rd.
Hemel Hempstead
Herts, England HP3 OA9
Author, Canvas Embroidery, *published by Merehurst Ltd., London*

Doug MacChestney
45140 Merritt St.
King City, CA 93930
Sporran maker

Karen Madigan
3 Paradise Close
Old Bar, NSW 2430
Australia
Fiber artist; mail order tassel earrings

Anita Mayer
1379 Islewood Dr.
Anacortes, WA 98221
Clothing design workshops; author of handwoven clothing books

David and Bobbe McClure
c/o Uncle Burley's
P.O. Box 1380
Van Horn, TX 79855
Mail order brooms and brushes

Merwitz Textiles
415 W. Huron
River North
Chicago, IL 60610
Custom designed tassels for the trade

Vima de Marchi Micheli
2561 Morley Way
Sacramento, CA 95864
Tassel and needlework teacher

Jock Montgomery
Box 1758
Surrey Dr.
Hemlock Farm
Hawley, PA 18428

Outer Edge Expeditions
222 So. Figueroa St., Suite 1311
Los Angeles, CA 90012
Specializes in small group expeditions to remote areas. Discover how I found out why llamas have tassels in their ears.

Pacific Circle Arts
1026 Murray St.
Berkeley, CA 94710
Primitive art of New Guinea

Carol Perrenoud
16510 S.W. Edminston Rd.
Wilsonville, OR 97070-9514
Beading teacher; mail order beads

John Ragsdale
95 1/2 Broad St.
Charleston, SC 29401
Wood finials and tassels (to order)

Jim Rankin
P.O. Box 07571
Milwaukee, WI 53207
Tassel collector; documentalist

Gerda Rasmussen
1227 Sunset Cliffs
San Diego, CA 92107
Needlework workshops

Barbara Jeanne Rice
P.O. Box 736
Colfax, WA 99111
Fiber artist

Tony and Gail Rossi
P.O. Box 1026
Bluelake, CA 95525
Tours to China; author of Chinese textile books

Warren Rossiter
180 2nd Ave.
Riddell, CA 95562
Jewelry maker

Tobias Schneebaum
463 West St. #627A
New York, NY 10014
Author; adventure traveler

Carolyn Schultz
Bethel College
North Newton, KS 67117
Author, Wheat Weaving Made Easy; mail order supply for wheat

Joan Schulze
808 Piper Ave.
Sunnyvale, CA 94087
Quilt and needlework workshops; textile commissions

Jeffrey and Katrina Seaton
30 Anacapa St.
Santa Barbara, CA 93101
Wood sculpture commissions

Marie Q. Sims
18330 Jefferson Hwy.
Baton Rouge, LA 70817
Textile artist

John Skare
Box 51
Bricelyn, MN 56014
Fiber artist

Vera Skipper
1420 Mt. Dandenong Rd.
Australia, 3767
Fiber artist

Society Expeditions
3131 Elliot Ave., Suite 700
Seattle, WA 98121
Cruise to primitive cultures in isolated areas—in comfort. White table cloths, five-course meals, the same bed every night, but exciting zodiac exploring during the day.

Vini Sozzani
5021 Old Cliffs Rd.
San Diego, CA 92120
Fiber artist

Tourist Authority of Thailand
3440 Wilshire Blvd., Suite 1100
Los Angeles, CA 90010
The land of smiling faces, golden places, and tassels everywhere

Noni Welch
150 Downey, #4
San Francisco, CA 94117

Greg Wells
Cindy Solek
223 W. San Francisco
Santa Fe, NM 87501
Boot maker; leather coats; commissions

Richard and Florie Wezelman
1750 Capistrano
Berkeley, CA 94707
African imports

Karen Whitney
7954 El Capitan Dr.
La Mesa, CA 92307
Beadwork

Wooden Porch Books
Rte. 1, Box 262
Middlebourne, WV 26149
Mail order source for old needlework books and magazines

Rita Zerull
Box 27532
Escondido, CA 92027
Fiber artist; teacher

Ellen Holt, Houlès, Scalamandré, and **Corona Decor** tassels are available through home furnishing stores and decorators.

Beth Karjala and Noni Welch don't know each other, but judging from their incredible tassels, they think alike.

Left: Noni Welch created a birthday tassel for me by attaching old watch bands, and hearts found at the flea market, to an antique salt-shaker.

Right: Beth Karjala's tassel is suspended from a copper pot-scrubber stuffed into a funnel. Chains are wired to the scrubber, and a personal hardware store dangles from them.

Gratitudes

It always astonished me how many people an author thanked in this section. I used to think, "I don't even know that many people, let alone people who would help me!" Yet here I am at this point, and my list is long. I apologize if I have unintentionally forgotten one of you. I wasn't aware when I started that the day would come when I felt so incredibly grateful for each person's help, support, and encouragement. Your warmth, sharing, energy, and even craziness is deeply appreciated.

A huge bouquet for my illustrator, Gail Gandolfi, who filled in at the last minute and who labored hard to understand the fiber world. When she started, she didn't know a tassel from a turnip, and now she finds tassels everywhere. A hug to Doris Hoover, who co-authored my first tassel book and talked me into this one.

My wonderful family contributed immensely—my husband most of the time. My traveling daughter, Noni, found tassels and took photos from the Himalayas across China to Czechoslovakia and enlisted her friends, Jock Montgomery and Frank Arnold, to help. My son, Steve, did a yeoman's job—long-distance—of computer aid every time I got in trouble. My daughter-in-law, Jennifer, can make her Apple do anything—including braids! And if that's not enough, my sons and their wives also contributed four grandchildren. I thank you and love you all dearly.

An enormous thank you to all the artists and photo contributors who generously loaned their work. Most are busy professionals who took the time (which often entailed considerable correspondence) to contribute. I trust they will be pleased with the results. Their names and addresses are included in the Resources section if you too would like to thank them. There could not have been a book without them.

I was fortunate to spend a day at the Field Museum in Chicago, a wonderland of tassels from the far corners of the world. I owe this special experience to Dr. Harold Voris, Dorothy Roder, and Christine Gross.

A sincere thanks also to Dr. Peter Kedit of the Sarawak Museum, Malaysia, who educated me by mail about headhunters, and to Brother Dom Garramone O.S.B., who reached into the heavens to send me bits of tassel lore. Betsey Warrick deserves a big tassel for her dedication to Mien refugees and for allowing me to photograph their work.

Anyone who tries the directions in this book for tying knots and braiding braids will be as indebted as I am to the Sacramento Fiber Guild and the Black Sheep Handweavers Guild, as well as to Maggie, Ann, Shirley, Joan, Louise, and Linda. Their fingers may still be sore.

Lois Muller, Linda Colsh, Carrie Arnold, Margery Williams, Sara Drower, Margot Carter Blair, and Jim Rankin—thanks. You were so helpful; I hope we meet some day.

A special thank you to friends who added bits and pieces of love and tassels at just the right time: Barbara Arthur, Mary Black, Shirley Burns, Linda Doherty, Carla Dole, Marilyn Green, Sara Louise Faustman, Fran Forsyth, Louise Goodrich, Selma Grossman, Gen Guracar, Joy May Hilden, Chris Martin, Hanne-Lore Nepote, Anne Steinhardt, Betty Stuntz, Budd Symes, Caroline Symes, and Jean Thompson.

I wish you all the biggest and brightest of tassels.

Nancy Rolph Welch

P.O. Box 620332
Woodside, CA 94062

Clockwise from top:
Tiny personal tassels
that hold a special place
in the author's heart.
One adorns a bread-
dough heart sent to her
from Czechoslovakia
by her daughter. The
stuffed fabric heart,
electric switch (You
Turn Me On), and yarn
tassels were made for
her by a very dear
friend. The string of
satin charms is a
reminder of a Chinese
adventure.

Bibliography

Anderson, Marilyn. *Guatemalan Textiles Today*. New York: Watson-Guptill Publications, 1978.

Barnard, Nicholas. *Living with Decorative Textiles: Tribal Art From Africa, Asia and the Americas*. New York: Doubleday & Co., 1989.

Blum, Stella. *Everyday Fashions of the Twenties As Pictured in Sears and Other Catalogs*. New York: Dover, 1982.

Boger, Louise Ade. *Furniture Past & Present*. New York: Doubleday & Co., 1966.

Boudet, Pierre, and Gomond, Bernard. *La Passementerie*. Paris: Dessain et Tolra, 1981.

Cahlander, Adele; Rowe, Ann Pollard; Zorn, Elayne. *Sling Braiding of the Andes*. Monograph IV. Boulder, Colorado: Colorado Fiber Center, 1965.

Campbell, Joseph. *The Way of the Animal Powers*. Vol.1 *Historical Atlas of World Mythology*. London: Summerfield, 1983.

Coleman, Elizabeth Ann. *The Opulent Era: Fashions of Worth, Doucet and Pingat*. New York: Thames and Hudson, 1989.

Conn, Richard. *Native American Art in the Denver Art Museum*. Seattle, Wash.: University of Washington Press, 1979.

Daniels, Ger. *Folk Jewelry of the World*. New York: Rizzoli Intl., 1989.

Davenport, Millie. *Book of Costume*. New York: Crown, 1948.

Day, Cyrus Lawrence. *Quipus and Witches' Knots*. Lawrence, Kansas: The University of Kansas Press, 1967.

Dinger, Charlotte. *Art of the Carousel*. Green Village, N.J.: Carousel Art Inc., 1984.

Dockstader, Frederick. *Song of the Loom*. New York: Hudson Hills Press, 1987.

Erté. *Erté at Ninety-five: The Complete New Graphics*. New York: E.P. Dutton, 1987.

Erté. *Erté Fashions*. London: Academy Editions, 1972.

Fairservis, Jr., Walter A. *Costumes of the East*. Old Greenwich, Conn.: The Chatham Press, Inc., 1971.

Franklyn, Julian and Tanner, John. *An Encyclopaedic Dictionary of Heraldy*. Oxford: Pergamon Press, 1969.

Haertig, Evelyn. *Antique Combs and Purses*. Carmel, Calif.: Gallery Graphics, 1983.

Halifax, Joan. *Shaman: The Wounded Healer*. New York: Thames Hudson, 1988.

Hart, Clive. *Kites: An Historical Survey*. Winchester, Mass.: Faber & Faber, 1967.

Hecht, Ann. *The Art of the Loom: Weaving, Spinning, and Dyeing Across the World*. New York: Rizzoli Intl., 1990.

Heim, Bernard Bruno. *Heraldry in the Catholic Church: Its Origins, Customs and Laws*. Atlantic Highlands, N.J.: Humanities Press, 1978.

Hinds, Anne Dion. *Grab the Brass Ring: The American Carousel*. New York: Crown Publishers, Inc., 1990.

Hughes, Therle. *English Domestic Needlework*. New York: The Macmillan Company, 1961.

Jefferson, Louise E. *The Decorative Arts of Africa*. New York: Viking Press, 1973.

Jones, Barbara and Bill Howell. *Popular Arts of the First World War*. New York: McGraw-Hill, 1972.

Jue, David F. *Chinese Kites: How to Make and Fly Them*. Rutland, Vt.: Charles E. Tuttle, 1967.

Kalter, Johannes. *The Arts and Crafts of Turkestan*. New York: Thames and Hudson, 1985.

Kirk, Malcolm. *Man As Art: New Guinea*. New York: Viking Press, 1981.

Kurth, Willie, ed. *Complete Woodcuts of Albrecht Durer*. New York, Dover Books, 1963.

Lester, Kathrine Morris and Oerke, Bess Viola. *Illustrated History of Those Frills and Furbelows of Fashion Which Have Come to Be Known as Accessories of Dress*. Peoria, Ill.,: Manual Arts Press, 1940.

Lewis, Henry Morgan. *The Indian Journals: 1859-62*. Ann Arbor: University of Michigan, 1959.

Lewis, Paul and Elaine. *Peoples of the Golden Triangle: Six Tribes in Thailand*. New York: Thames and Hudson Inc. 1984.

Mack, John. *Ethnic Jewelry*. New York: Abrams, 1988.

Melegari, Vezio. *Regiments*. Milan: Rizolli, 1968.

Meyer, Franz S. *Handbook of Ornament*. New York: Dover Books, 1892.

Nicolson, Sir Harold. *Kings, Courts and Monarchy*. New York: Simon and Schuster, Inc., 1963.

O'Neale, Lila M. *Textiles of Highland Guatemala*. Washington, DC: Carnegie Institution of Washington, 1945.

Oka, Hideyuki. *How to Wrap Five More Eggs: Traditional Japanese Packaging*. New York & Tokyo: Weatherhill, 1975.

Osborne, Lilly de Jongh. *Indian Crafts of Guatemala and El Salvador*. Norman, Okla.: University of Oklahoma Press, 1965.

Piggott, Juliet. *Japanese Mythology: Library of The World's Myths and Legends*. New York: Peter Bedrick Books, 1969.

Priestley, J. B. T*he Edwardians*. New York: Harper & Row, Inc., 1970.

Racinet, Albert. *Historical Encyclopedia of Costume*. New York: Facts on File, 1988.

Smith, Bradley. *The USA: A History in Art*. New York: Thomas Crowell, 1977.

Streeter, Tal. T*he Art of the Japanese Kite*. New York: John Weatherhill, 1974.

Thornton, Peter. *Seventeenth Century Interior Decoration in England, France & Holland*. New Haven: Yale University, 1978.

Tilke, Max. *Costume Patterns and Designs*. New York: Hasting House Publishers, 1974.

White, Palmer. *Poiret*. New York: Clarkson N. Potter, Inc., 1973.

Wilcox, R. Turner. *Folk and Festival Costume of the World*. New York: Charles Scribner's Sons, 1977.

Wilcox, R. Turner. *Mode in Costume*. New York: Macmillan, 1974.

Wilson, Jean. *Weaving is Creative*. New York: Van Nostrand, 1972.

Woodcock, Thomas and John M. Robinson. *The Oxford Guide to Heraldry*. New York: Oxford University Press, 1990.

Zigrosser, Carl. *Medicine and the Artist*. New York: Dover, 1970.

Magazines: Courtesy of Wooden Porch Books, Middlebourne, W. Va.
   Peterson's, 1862.
   Journal Des Demoiselles, France, 1845.
   Demorest's, 1889.
   Harper's Bazaar, Jan. 6, Jan. 13, Feb. 24, Aug. 17, 1872.

Museum of the Fur Trade Quarterly, Winter 1969.

Once a Week, Vol IV, December 1860, June 1861. (Courtesy of Jim Rankin)

Photography Credits

Illustrations by Gail Gandolfi

Illustrations labeled "SB" by Shirley Burns

Photographs not otherwise credited
were graciously provided by the artists
featured in the Tassel Gallery and by
Ed and Nancy Welch.

A rainbow of finely crafted tassels from Corona Decor

Index